SCHMITTOU

A Grand Slam In Baseball, Business, And Life

by
Larry Woody

Eggman Publishing Company
Nashville, Tennessee

Also by Larry Woody

A Dixie Farewell: The Life and Times of Chucky Mullins
Pure Sterling: The Sterling Marlin Story

SCHMITTOU

*A Grand Slam
In Baseball,
Business,
And Life*

ISBN: 1-886371-33-4

Cover Design: Bill Tyler

Eggman Publishing Company
3012 Hedrick Street
Nashville, TN 37203

For interviews and other information, call
615-386-0133
1-800-396-4626

DEDICATION

To the family of Larry Schmittou—his wife, Shirley, and their children Debbie, Ronnie, Mike, Susan, and Steve—whose faith and support have been unwavering.

And to the memory of Jane Ann (Janie) and Egbert Schmittou, who instilled in their son the qualities he credits for his success, both in life and baseball.

From the author, a debt of gratitude to the late Lon (Bud) Burns, who, during 40 years of battling late games and early deadlines as a sports writer and editor with the *Tennessean*, never hesitated to put aside his smoldering stogie to lend a hand to the new kid in the sports department.

Were it not for their influence and assistance, this book would not have been possible.

FOREWORD

I became acquainted with Larry Schmittou during our coaching days at Vanderbilt. We became good friends and have remained good friends all through the years.

I really don't know what, exactly, it was that drew Schmittou and me together at Vanderbilt. He coached baseball and did some football recruiting, and I was strictly in football. But we were around each other a lot, of course, with Schmittou involved in the football program. And I loved baseball, always have since I was a kid. So I went to a lot of games and Schmittou and I began to hang out together. We traveled together, had a lot of fun, and shared a lot of laughs.

On one hand, I guess there couldn't be two more different people than we are. I grew up in New Jersey, while Schmittou grew up in Tennessee on some little farm. But even though I came from the city and Schmittou from the country, we shared a love of sports. That was one thing we had in common.

Then, too, I think our personalities are very similar. We're both very competitive; we want to win in anything we do whether it's baseball, football, or some of our famous gin-rummy games.

I remember how much I admired the job he did as Vanderbilt's baseball coach. He took over a program that really wasn't much and built it from nothing into an SEC championship team. That's one reason I liked to hang around Schmittou: I liked to study his style, the way he did things.

And I think he did the same with me and my work with the football team. We learned from each other.

We share a very similar philosophy: we work hard, set high goals, and try to do whatever is necessary to achieve them. We both love to win.

As I kept up with Schmittou over the years, I wasn't a bit surprised to hear and read about his success in professional baseball. He knows the game, loves the game, and is a dedicated worker. When Schmittou makes up his mind he's going to do something, he doesn't stop until he gets it done. He would have been a success in anything he set his mind to; it just happened to be baseball.

As competitive as he is, Schmittou is really a nice guy. He was always ready to help out, to do someone a favor. All they had to do was ask. And he's still that way. If I need something today, all I have to do is give him a call.

That may be what I admire most about Schmittou: he's very loyal. If he's your friend, he's your friend for life. I'm proud to say he's one of mind.

Bill Parcells
Head Coach, New England Patriots

INTRODUCTION

Roger Kahn, in his classic *Boys of Summer*, wrote "The noontime of the American Dream glows briefly."

Larry Schmittou dared to seize the moment.

Schmittou is a colorful, controversial character whose name has become synonymous with baseball in Nashville and other minor-league environs around the nation.

Born in 1940, Schmittou experienced a hardscrabble upbringing in a section of town he calls Lower West Nashville, where pioneers once fought and died.

Schmittou's father, Egbert, was disabled by nerve gas in World War I. As a youngster Schmittou attended Nashville Vols games at old Sulphur Dell with his mother, Jane Ann. They walked a mile to the bus stop, rode to the ball park, took the bus back to the stop, and walked home—after Janie Schmittou had worked all day to help support her family.

That early baseball nurturing led Schmittou to sandlot ball, first as a player and later as the city's most celebrated coach. After earning his degree from Peabody College, Schmittou coached in junior high and high school before becoming Vanderbilt's first full-time baseball coach.

Schmittou also served as a Vanderbilt football recruiter, where he became close friends with Bill Parcells, who would later find fame as an NFL coach.

Schmittou eventually became disenchanted with some of the more sordid sides of intercollegiate athletics and, weary of trying to support a wife and five children on a $14,000 coach's salary, decided to seek his fortune bringing professional baseball back to Nashville.

He talked the city into leasing him a vacant softball lot and worked tirelessly to attract investors, eventually mortgaging his own home to generate capital for his Greer Stadium dream.

"I've laid my head on a pillow $5 million in debt, knowing I was one rainout away from not being able to meet a payroll," says Schmittou. "Believe me—you don't sleep well."

Schmittou eventually succeeded, building a record-smashing minor-league dynasty through sheer will and determination.

In the process he would make money, lose money, gain friends, create enemies, defy convention, and earn a national reputation for being innovative, old-fashioned, cautious, creative, witty, grumpy, personable, cantankerous, outgoing, private, selfish, and giving.

Not the descriptive inconsistencies, the character paradoxes, the enigmas of persona.

Therein lies the mystique of Larry Schmittou. He is at once unassumingly simple and profoundly complex—not unlike the game of baseball itself.

"Larry Schmittou probably knows more people than anybody in Nashville," says longtime friend Jim Fyke, "but very few people know Larry."

"I don't mind making it hard for people to get me pegged, to figure me out," says Schmittou. "I like to keep 'em guessing."

In baseball lingo, it's known as not being able to hit what you can't see.

Schmittou has never dodged controversy. He has vocally opposed virtually every new professional sports venture that came along that might compete with his beloved Sounds for media attention and fan interest.

"I don't apologize," says Schmittou. "I'm in the baseball business and I look out for baseball. Anything that goes head-to-head with baseball is the competition. I'm no different from those who judge me. The morning newspaper in our town never refers to the evening paper by name, and I haven't seen McDonald's suggesting that people eat at Burger King."

There is another side to Schmittou, a gentler, less-combative side that the public rarely sees. One season the wife of Sounds announcer Bob Jamison gave birth to a seriously ill baby boy. Schmittou instructed Jamison to take a fully paid leave of absence for as long as he wanted. When the child tragically lost its struggle for life, Schmittou secretly paid for the funeral.

"Larry does things like that all the time," says one close associate. "But the media and the public seldom know about them."

This is the story of the frolicking ride—of triumph and turmoil, good times and bad, friendships and feuds—of Nashville's king of diamonds. It affords a behind-the-curtain peek at the workings of a successful pro baseball franchise, some of the game's colorful characters, and most of all, the man who is arguably the single most influential sports figure in Nashville's history.

It is, as they say, a work in progress, because Schmittou's story is far from complete. In the words of the venerable dugout philosopher Yogi Berra, "It ain't over till it's over."

Larry Schmittou has a lot of innings left.

Chapter I

Mama and
the Ball Park

"The apple doesn't fall far from the tree."

L arry Schmittou, who earned a reputation in baseball circles as an unpredictable, keep 'em guessing chance-taker, has been springing surprises on people all his life—starting with his own parents, Egbert and Jane Ann.

"I was an accident," says Schmittou of his arrival on July 19, 1940.

"My father was 46 and my mother was 44. I was the fifth of five children and my oldest brother had already graduated from high school when I was born. I wasn't planned.

"I was born at home, in what I call Lower West Nashville, about five miles from downtown, near the old Tennessee State Prison. Our neighborhood had a tough reputation back then— it was so tough the prisoners were afraid to escape at night."

The Schmittou residence, at 5904 Robertson Road, was the original homeplace of James Robertson, an early pioneer who is known as the Father of Tennessee.

"There is a historical marker there that says Robertson's original home was burned down by Indians," says Schmittou. "Two of his children, who were killed by Indians, are buried on the back of my dad's property. That's where Robertson Road got its name."

A tough neighborhood with a tough history. A fitting place for a man like Egbert Schmittou to try to scratch out a grim postwar living. Egbert, whose formal education ended after the third grade, had been severely disabled by nerve gas while serving in World War I. He subsequently developed tuberculosis. Although physically impaired, Egbert Schmittou did his best to help his wife and children run their 12-acre truck farm and pick up whatever other work was available.

"We raised hogs, a couple of cows, and, oh gosh, always a bunch of stinking, filthy chickens," says Schmittou. "I had to chop weeds out of the garden, take care of cows and pigs, mow grass . . . I did all the usual kinds of farm chores. We didn't have a tractor; we plowed with an old mule.

"In my younger years I can remember my father working at McCord's, a little grocery store across the street. After he developed TB the state health department made us stop selling milk and then they made us sell our cows. They began testing my dad every 30 days or so to monitor his TB. Each time he tested positive he had to go into Veteran's Hospital.

"After the third time he tested positive, they made him stop working at the grocery store because TB was so contagious back then.

"So what little outside income he had been able to generate was now gone. My dad drew a small pension from the DAV but it wasn't much.

"For years my dad would not allow the morning paper on our property and it wasn't until I was grown that I found out why. It was because the morning paper supported the Democrats, and Franklin Delano Roosevelt had suspended the DAV pension checks.

"Looking back, I guess my mom and dad and older brothers and sister almost starved to death. But by the time I came along, my brothers and sister were out working to help supplement our family's income. They all worked, and most of the money came back home to help buy food. Compared with them—and thanks to them—my standard of living was pretty good."

To help make ends meet, Schmittou and his mother and father did part-time work packaging needles.

"Two of my older brothers, Leo and Harry, worked at the National Life & Accident Insurance Company," Schmittou explains, "where for years the company gave away packs of needles as a promotion.

"My brothers got us jobs gluing needles onto the little cardboard packets they came in. We'd glue 10 million or more of those needles onto little folders. We were paid $1 per thousand needles. All of us did it. Me. My dad. My mother.

"To break the monotony and to make it seem like fun, we'd have a contest to see who could do it the fastest. I did a thousand needles in 45 minutes to win the first contest. But my brother Harry threatened to fire me because not all the needles were on straight on the card. When you folded it up some of the needles were poking out and they would stick whoever picked up the pack.

"So I had to slow down. It took about an hour per thousand to do it right. So that's about what we earned, one dollar an hour, gluing needles. It doesn't sound like much now, but I can remember how much every one of those dollars meant to us back then."

Schmittou has especially fond memories of his mother, whom he describes as "the hardest-working person I ever knew.

"I called her Mama and everybody else called her Janie. I learned my work ethic from her. She was about 4-foot-11, 110 pounds, a Bible-quoting, foot-washing Primitive Baptist who could work on the farm all day long, doing the work of any grown man, and never give out. She was the toughest little woman who ever lived.

"When I was 15 years old, I hauled rocks in a wheelbarrow and Mama, at age 59, built the foundation on our house to build me a room of my own.

"We didn't own a car, and my mother often walked five miles to town and back when she had to buy something. She could have walked two miles to 46th and Charlotte and caught a bus on in and saved herself three miles, but she refused to spend the 25 cents or whatever the bus cost back then. She walked the whole way."

That wasn't all the walking Janie Schmittou did. After working all week on the farm, doing her share of packing needles at night, caring for her family, and attending church, she still somehow found the time and energy to take her youngest son to Sulphur Dell Baseball Park to watch the Nashville Vols play. Schmittou is named after Larry Gilbert, the Vols manager.

"We didn't get to go much, usually only on a Sunday afternoon," Schmittou says. "Oh, every now and then, if I ding-donged at her, Mama might take me during the week if she had the time.

"In order to go, we had to walk to 46th and Charlotte, about two miles from home. We'd catch a bus from there to Sulphur Dell. After the game we'd take the bus back to 46th and Charlotte, get off, and walk the rest of the way home.

"It wasn't that my Dad didn't want to go to the games, but his TB limited what he was able to do. So my mama took me to baseball games."

It was during those boyhood visits to Sulphur Dell with his mother that Schmittou began to develop a love affair with baseball that would become the focal point of his entire life.

"About then I began to collect baseball cards and my interest in the game grew from there," he says.

Janie Schmittou, who had been forced to terminate her formal schooling after business college in Bowling Green, Kentucky, was a fierce believer in the value of an education. She was bound and determined to see her children get the very best available.

"My older brother Leo was an honor student at Central High and had visions of becoming a doctor, and my next-oldest brother, Harry, was also an excellent student," says Schmittou.

"But World War II came along and their college plans were interrupted. My sister, Gladys, got married and quit school. My brother John, who was next to me, wanted to be a musician and didn't want to go to college. Then he got into the Korean Conflict.

"So that left me, and my mother kind of made me her special project in terms of getting an education. My mama had already taught me how to read and write before I got to elementary school, so when I got there they put me in the second grade right off.

"I later hated that, because I was interested in sports, and that meant that I was a year younger and smaller than the rest of the kids in my class. And I wasn't very good anyway."

When it came time for Schmittou to enter high school, his mother decided the neighborhood school wasn't good enough for her prize pupil.

"Where we lived we weren't inside the old city limits, so I was supposed to go to Bellevue High," says Schmittou. "But Bellevue didn't have Latin, which my mother felt I should take, along with at least three years of mathematics. So my mother made up her mind that I would go to Cohn.

"But to go there, I had to request to take another course Bellevue didn't offer. So my mother enrolled me in orchestra, as a fiddle player; I hated it. During my first year, Larry Roberts, who was the brother of one of my best friends, was as bad a fiddle player as I was. We had a really good violinist named Roby Ann Story who later wound up with the New York Symphony.

"John Bright was our orchestra teacher, and at the end of our first year we were going on a recital to Murfreesboro. Mr.

Bright called Roberts and me into his office and said to us, 'You guys are in the orchestra, so you have to go, too. Here's what I want you to do: you look at Robyann's bow and when Roby Ann's bow goes up, I want yours to go up. Just make sure your bows do not touch the strings. If you'll do that and agree not to sign up for orchestra again next year, I'll give you a B.' That's how my music career ended.

"My mother placed a great deal of emphasis on education. She kept close watch on my grades. My first year I made Bs, a few As, but I had a couple of buddies who were making better grades because they signed up for easier courses. It's easier to make a good grade in chorus than in Latin II.

"So, at the start of my junior year my mother asked me what I was going to take. I told her geometry, Spanish, and chemistry, but when I got to school I didn't sign up for geometry and Spanish. I put down bookkeeping and typing.

"But I made a fatal mistake. I didn't take any books home for a couple of weeks. Each day my mother would ask, 'Have you done your homework?' I had to do it before I did my needles. I'd tell her I did it at school.

"One day I was in class and the principal, Mr. Rochelle, a tough educator whose son is now a state representative, called me to his office. I went in and there sat my mama. I knew I was in big-time trouble.

"She said, 'Why have you not signed up for geometry and Spanish?' I said I thought I needed those other courses.

"Her remedy was that I keep all those other courses, but I would also add geometry and Spanish, which put me two weeks behind going in. And she said if I did not make at least a B in everything I could not play sports. The rest she said she would take up with me when we got home. I knew what that meant.

Schmittou's parents kept a tight rein on their children's social life.

"Like I said, we lived in a pretty tough neighborhood and hanging around on the corner of 46th and Charlotte after a football game was a pretty big thing to do," he says.

"The kids didn't do anything back then; hanging out was just a status symbol. But I wasn't allowed to do it.

"My mother and father knew exactly how long it took to walk home from Cohn's Sykes Field, and at exactly 25 minutes after a practice or a game was over, I was expected to walk through that front door.

"When I was a junior in high school I decided I was going to hang out on the corner. So there I was, hanging out, and all at once I looked up and there was my mama—all 4-foot-11, 110 pounds, coming after me with a broom.

"Before I could move she hit me about eight times with that broom, grabbed me, and we started for home. But before we had gone two blocks she stopped and hugged me and said, 'You knew you weren't supposed to be there. Don't you ever do this again.' And I didn't."

Egbert Schmittou left the administration of punishment up to his wife.

"My daddy never whipped me," says Schmittou. "And when my mama whipped me, she used switches. She made me go get the switch, and the size of the switch depended on the degree of the offense.

"Once I hit my brother in the head with a croquet ball and I had to get a pretty good-sized switch that time. But the biggest switch I ever got was the first year I went out for football. I didn't like football and didn't want to play; I wanted to play baseball.

"But Eddie Adleman was the coach, and he said if you wanted to play baseball or basketball you had to play football.

"I had to get up early and do my farm chores. Football practice started at 6 in the morning and lasted until 10. Then we would go back at 2 and practice till dark during fall two-a-day practice.

"In order to be on time for morning practice, I had to get up at 4, go get the eggs, throw some feed over the fence for the cows, and start walking over to the practice field.

"We had a big old rooster and he'd always fan up at me when I went down there. I carried a stick, and one morning I was hurrying to get through my chores and get to practice. Well, I was already mad about having to go to football practice, so I swung my stick at him and accidentally broke his neck. He flopped around and died, and I just left him lying there and went on to practice.

"About four hours later I came dragging home, tired after being killed playing a sport I didn't want to play, and my daddy said, 'Boy, did you kill that rooster?'

"And I said, 'Yes sir, I did.'

"He turned to Mama and said, 'Make him go get the biggest switch out there.'

"Well, I brought three switches before she finally settled on the biggest one. There I was, a sophomore in high school, and I had to get that switch and drop my pants.

"I hadn't fully appreciated what that one mean old rooster meant to us and the rest of our chickens. He was our only rooster and I had wiped out a valuable asset. I guess that was my first lesson in the birds and the bees."

Janie Schmittou died on April 25, 1978, the day before her son's brand-new baseball team, the Nashville Sounds, took the field for the first time.

Schmittou was on a baseball field when he got news of his mother's death.

"I was coaching baseball at Vanderbilt at the time," he says, "and when I saw my wife, Shirley, come walking across the field toward me that afternoon, I knew what happened. Mama had had a series of strokes and had been bad off for about a year. So I knew what to expect.

"Shirley came out and told me Mama had died. I thought I'd be prepared for it when it happened, but I really wasn't. I went to the clubhouse and just sat there crying.

"I still think about her and miss her."

Egbert Schmittou died in 1986 at the age of 92, while his son was working as an executive with the Texas Rangers of the American League.

"My dad was awfully good to me," says Schmittou. "He taught me to make my own way, and he taught me never to break my word on anything.

"When I was in college I wanted to buy a car. It was a '52 Ford, the prettiest little car I'd ever seen in my life. Trouble was, it cost $300 and I didn't have $300. My daddy told me to go see Andy Gibson at Third National Bank in West Nashville.

"I walked into Mr. Gibson's office, scared, not having any idea about how to borrow money. Mr. Gibson looked up and said, 'Who're you, boy?'

"I said, 'Larry Schmittou, sir.'

He said, 'Oh, you played up there at Cohn, didn't you?'

"And I said, 'Yes, sir.'

"He said, 'You Egbert's boy?'

"And I said, 'Yes, sir.'

"He said, 'How much money you want? Your daddy always paid me back, so I'll do this for you.'

"That was my credit check—my daddy, and his reputation for always paying his bills.

"My father also taught me not to waste money. He actually took it too far. Once, after my mother died, I went over to his house to visit him and he was sitting there watching television with nothing on the screen but a little white dot.

"I asked him what was wrong with the TV and he said he didn't know. So why didn't he get it fixed, or go buy a new TV? He said it would cost too much, and besides, there wasn't anything on worth watching, anyway. So he just left it like that.

"Everything I am, I owe to the lessons I learned from my mother and father," says Schmittou. "They taught me the value of hard work, honesty, and determination.

"I learned early on that I was not gifted in anything. If I wanted to get anything done, I'd better be prepared to out-work everybody else who wanted what I wanted. As it turned out, at first it was coaching, then it was marketing and whatever else came along.

"We were poor by most people's standards, but in terms of the values I learned, I was one the richest little boys in Nashville."

CHAPTER II
KING OF DIAMONDS

"Winning isn't everything, but it's in the top 5."

From the very beginning, baseball was the key that unlocked doors for Larry Schmittou.

"When I was a junior in high school I began coaching a Junior Knot Hole League team for kids 9 to 12," says Schmittou. "I was only 16 at the time, just four years older than the kids I was coaching. But I ended up with a good team and we won a lot of games, and that got me going as a coach. I loved to win.

"It was funny how it happened. Bobby Roberts, one of my best friends, and I had talked about coaching. Eddie Adleman, who was coach at Cohn High, called us into his office one day and said, 'I understand you guys want to coach. Why don't you go over and see Joe Troteman with the Junior Chamber? They're sponsoring a new league called Junior Knot Hole and they need volunteer coaches.'

"So Bobby and I went over and Mr. Troteman wound up giving us each a team at Cockrill Elementary School. Bobby and I were pretty good friends and we didn't know how to go about dividing up the little kids who had come out. Finally we decided the fairest way would be to pick two kids and let them choose the rest of the teams.

"I told Bobby he could pick first, and of course he picked the biggest kid in the class.

"All at once this little bitty kid—I'll never forget his name—Charlie Mosley, he comes running over to me and says, 'Get Harold Dierdorf! He's the best player!'

"So I yelled, 'Dierdorf!' As it turned out, Bobby had picked the biggest sissy in school. He picked his buddies, and Dierdorf picked all the good players.

"Even though I didn't know how to coach—didn't have any idea what I was doing—I won all but one game that season simply because I had the best players. I guess that was a good early lesson—good players make good coaches.

"But the bottom line was, I won, and I really loved it. I was hooked. And so I coached again the next year. That's what got me started as a coach."

While coaching his Junior Knot Hole team, Schmittou was also playing baseball—ingloriously, according to his account—at Cohn High.

"I was a pitcher, and most pitchers can't hit," he says. "I was unique; I couldn't do either very well."

That didn't stop Schmittou from nurturing dreams of some-day playing professionally.

"Despite all my mother's emphasis on education, I hadn't planned on going to college," he admits. "I realize now I didn't throw hard enough, but one couldn't tell me that back then. I was certain I would end up in the majors."

"After my senior year in high school there were a lot of tryout camps and I went to every one. I figured that in four or five years I'd be playing in the World Series.

"Finally that summer I went to a camp Pittsburgh was hold-ing in Kingsport, Tennessee. There were 10 or 12 of us who went from Nashville, and I thought we were signed. We had signed a piece of paper I thought was a contract, but I guess it was just a waiver in case we got hurt.

"Anyway, they paid our way up there and when I arrived there were about 200 other players in camp. We had uniforms that had 'Pirates' on the front and we played intersquad games for two or three days. I thought I was doing pretty good.

"But after about the third day this guy, one of the scouts, called me over, put his arm around my shoulder and said, 'Uh, son, you need to go to college.'

"My tryout was over, and so was my big-league dream."

Schmittou returned home to Nashville.

"I didn't know what I was going to do," he says. "My family barely had enough money to live on, let alone send me to college.

"While I was in high school I had joined the Key Club. Our principal, Mr. W. R. Rochelle, had recommended me for a little $300 scholarship the Kiwanis Club offered because I was good in math. I had kinda put it in the back of my mind, and when my pro-baseball bubble burst, I remembered that scholarship. I decided I'd try it.

"I didn't have a car, so I couldn't go out of town to school. I sure couldn't afford to go to Vanderbilt. There was Lipscomb but it was Church of Christ and my mother, bless her heart, wouldn't consider that—although Shirley, the woman I would wind up marrying, is a strong Church of Christ person.

"Anyway, that left Peabody College, which then, and I guess still is, a nationally famous teacher's college. I applied, got accepted, and suddenly figured something out: I didn't have enough money to go. Then came more of my luck—although I think 'luck' is something you have because you've done something to deserve it.

"The head person over the whole Knot Hole League was a man named Wesley Kinser, now a real estate developer. But his main job at the time was personnel director at the Ford Glass Plant. I told my story to Mr. Troteman, Mr. Troteman told my story to Mr. Kinser, and Mr. Kinser—who knew me because of my Knot Hole coaching—called and said they were hiring at the plant.

"I went over, but I was told I had to be 18 to be hired. I'd graduated from high school but I wasn't 18 yet because I'd skipped first grade. Mr. Kinser said he would give me a job in the plant cafeteria, where I didn't have to be 18 to work.

"So I worked in the cafeteria while I was waiting to turn 18 and made enough money to pay my first term's tuition at Peabody.

"Also, through the YMCA, I got a job coaching in their Gray-Y program, football and basketball, and helping teach swimming at the Y.

"Six months later, after I turned 18, Mr. Kinser got me a job in the plant. People at that time were killing to get a job at the Ford Glass Plant because they were paying over $4 an hour. Les Jamison, who became a prominent Nashville radio personality, was my foreman.

"They put me on the midnight shift, where I could work from 11 at night until 7 in the morning. That way I could work, go to school, and still coach—by that time I was coaching three different amateur teams and playing on one.

"My normal routine was to work from 11 p.m. to 7 a.m., rush home, take a shower, and go to college classes from 8 a.m. to 2 or 3 p.m. I'd return home, sleep three or four hours, get up and go coach one of my teams or play in a game, then go straight to work.

"If it had not been for the Ford Glass Plant, I could not have gone to college, and if it had not been for Knot Hole baseball I could not have gotten on at the plant. It all went back to baseball."

Despite his 40-hour weekly night shift and full load of college courses, Schmittou still made time to coach his Knot Hole team (ages 9–12), a Babe Ruth team (ages 13–15), and an American Legion team (ages 16–18). He also played in the Old City League.

"It was hard, but I looked on my coaching then as an apprenticeship," says Schmittou. "I wanted to coach and I wanted to win. And I won big-time."

Schmittou won over 500 games as a sandlot coach, 20 city championships, and eight state championships, and six of his teams went to national tournaments in their age bracket.

His reputation as a coaching whiz exceeded the boundaries of Nashville's sandlots, spreading statewide, regionally, and even nationally as he directed his teams to a series of national tournaments.

At the time Schmittou was developing a reputation as a top coach, he was also earning a reputation among some of his sandlot rivals as a ruthless competitor who would stop at nothing to win.

The most common complaint directed toward Schmittou in those days was that he would recruit the top players from other neighborhoods, thereby stocking his teams with superior talent.

"Yes, I did," he admits. "But that certainly was not against the rules. And I worked at it. And after I won some championships I didn't need to recruit. The top players came to me. They wanted to play on my teams. I got a reputation as a great recruiter but I really didn't have to recruit. I probably recruited less than any coach in town. After a while, all I had to do was make a phone call."

Jim Fyke, who has been one of Schmittou's closest friends since he began working with the Metro Parks system in the 1960s, attributes much of Schmittou's amazing sandlot success to his simply out-working opposing coaches.

"When all the other volunteer coaches were trying to hold down a job or be with their families, or just rest, Schmittou was figuring out a way to beat them," says Fyke.

"He is as intense a competitor on and off the field as I've ever known. He'll always try to stay a step ahead of everyone."

As for Schmittou's lack of popularity among some of his fellow coaches: "We usually don't like the guy who keeps beating us," notes Fyke. "I don't know if Schmittou was disliked personally or just because of what he stood for: winning. He didn't care what they thought; all he cared about was winning."

Actually Schmittou states that his closest friends during this time were the people he coached against.

One of Schmittou's most interesting experiences as a coach didn't occur on a baseball field; it came aboard a train bound for Albuquerque.

"In 1965 my Connie Mack team won the regionals and we were headed for the World Series in New Mexico," says Schmittou. "We had planned to fly out—which, at age 25, would have been my first plane ride—but there was an air strike so we had to take the train most of the way. We only got to fly from Albuquerque to Farmington.

"I had some great players on that team—two Carter boys, Roy and Ray, Sam Ewing, Jim and Mike Mondelli, among others. So we're on the train, and somewhere out in Texas we decide to have a poker game to break the monotony. We're playing with matches for a quarter of a penny a point. The most anybody could have lost would have been about a quarter.

"So we're playing and the train pulls into a stop and several people get off. We don't pay any attention until all of a sudden a sheriff walks on and announces that he's going to arrest me and my whole team—including Mike Mondelli, who is now a judge.

"It wasn't a joke. Some passenger who got off had told a policeman inside the station that a poker game was going on the train, and the sheriff had been called.

"I tried to explain that we were playing for fun. I was sweating. I was there with a bunch of 16-to-18-year-old boys, being threatened with arrest for gambling. I'm thinking Mr. Mondelli will kill me if I ever get back home. Somehow I convinced the sheriff that we're innocent and he let us go.

"Of the boys on that team who were gambling, two are now preachers and one is a judge. I could have ruined three careers right there—not counting mine.

"It's funny now, but it sure wasn't funny that day with that sheriff standing there over me."

As a senior at Peabody College, Schmittou did his student teaching at Julia Green Elementary School, with his eye on an eventual position at Hillwood High, where some of his summer-league players attended.

"I applied for a teaching and coaching job in the Davidson County school system and at the ripe old age of 21 I was hired. I wanted to go to Hillwood, but a listing of assignments appeared in the paper, saying I was going to Haywood Elementary," recalls Schmittou. "I was determined I didn't want to go there, because they had only grades one through six and no athletic programs.

"I called Mr. Carter, the headmaster at Montgomery Bell Academy (a private school, considered one of Nashville's most exclusive) where I had done some part-time coaching, to see about maybe getting on full-time.

"In the meantime I was coaching a Babe Ruth All-Star team, and one of my players was Bill Waters, whose father, Hugh, was assistant superintendent of the old city school system.

"One day after practice Hugh came up to me and said, 'Congratulations on your new teaching job at Haywood.'

"I said, 'Thank you, but I'm not going to take it. I want to coach, and I'm not going to any elementary school. I'll go back to the Ford Glass Plant before I'll do that.'

"Mr. Waters said, 'How would you like to be the head coach of football, basketball, and track at Bailey Junior High?'

"I said, 'I'd like that.'

"And he said, 'You've got it.'

"Bailey consisted of grades seven through nine and had a long history of being a great basketball school. It was big in sports and that's what I was interested in."

So Schmittou took the position at Bailey Junior High, where, he says, "I learned a great lesson that I've always kept in mind in anything I did: Never follow a legend. That's what I did at Bailey, where I followed Frank Rutherford.

"From day one it was, 'Mr. Rutherford did it this way,' or, 'Mr. Rutherford did not do it this way.'

"He had coached everything, was a super-nice person, and still is. He and I used to play golf together. But he had won more games, more championships, more everything than anybody in the history of junior high sports.

"Not only had he won everything there was to win, he had been at Bailey for so many years that he'd coached the parents of many of my players. He was a legend, and I could never top that, no matter what I did. I learned a good, hard lesson there: It's hard to follow a legend, especially in sports.

Schmittou's three years at Bailey were, well, interesting.

"Bailey had a great basketball tradition, but they were just getting their football program going," he says. "Back then nobody except North High was fielding a junior high football team and they were understandably the best around.

"Well, we had 17 or 18 kids come out for our first football team. We played a couple of games against some teams who were just starting up, like us, and got beat by only seven, maybe 14 points. Then we played Howard, and in that game they kicked off to us and we got the ball on the 20. It never got past the 30. There must have been 30 fumbles in that game and we won 7–0. So now we're feeling pretty good. We've beaten somebody.

"Then we played North. Like I said, they had had a team for a while, and they were good. They had a back named DePasquel, a ninth-grader who played on the varsity. Nobody could stop him. At the end of the first quarter the score was something like 28 them, 0 us.

"Not only were we getting killed on the scoreboard, we had a kid get hurt, and that put us down to about 13 players. We had a little guy, I think his name was Sircy, and I yelled, 'Sircy, go in.' But we couldn't find him. We started looking around for Sircy—by now the score is about 35–0—and finally we find him hiding under the bleachers. He was sitting on his helmet, so he wouldn't have to go into the game. I can't say I blamed him.

"Finally, in the middle of the third quarter, their coach, Gene Pilkerton, looked across the field at us and hollered, 'Have you all had enough?'

"We waved back and yelled, 'Yep. That's it.'

"We loaded up and got out of there, and Sircy never had to go in. That ended his football career that day."

From Bailey Schmittou moved up to the high school ranks at Goodlettsville.

"As a summer vacation relief person, I was working at the Ford Glass Plant where I'd worked for six straight years while I was going to school, teaching, and coaching," says Schmittou. "I was making more working the midnight shift for 10 weeks than I made all year teaching and coaching.

"One day my wife called me at the plant and said the school board wanted me to come down for an interview. So I went down and Tommy Griffith and John Younger and Richard Graves were there. They had showed up to interview for football coaching positions, too.

"The only two jobs that were known to be open were the Cumberland High football job and the Overton High basketball job.

"Richard and John both wanted football jobs. I didn't want football. It interfered with my coaching summer baseball. Once I learned what was open, I wanted the Overton basketball job. But I figured Tommy would get it because he had more years in service. He's still there, going to state tournaments.

"When I went in for my interview, the only thing we talked about was the Cumberland High football job. Then I left and went back to work.

"The next morning, Bob Teitlebaum, a sports writer friend with the *Tennessean*, called me and said, 'Congratulations on your new coaching job.'

"I kinda greeted it with mixed feelings. I said something

like 'Well, I hope coaching football won't interfere with my baseball coaching.'

"And Teitlebaum informed me that I wasn't going to be coaching football; I was head basketball coach at Goodlettsville. Goodlettsville had never been mentioned in my interview.

"Paul Burgess, who was the Goodlettsville coach, had been named principal at Howard High School, which triggered the job opening. So I became basketball coach at Goodlettsville and was also assistant football coach. Metro had a rule that you could be the head coach in only one sport, so I didn't get to coach baseball at Goodlettsville. I helped out, but I was never the head coach of my preferred sport.

"Miles Frost, our head football coach at Goodlettsville, had a slight heart attack after our first two games of my third year, and Mr. Sircy, our principal, asked me to coach the rest of the season.

"I had a genius at quarterback, Bill Burton, a straight-A student. He knew more about football than I did, so I just told Bill to call whatever plays he wanted to, and we went undefeated for our last eight games.

"As far as I know, I'm the only football coach in the history of Metro who never lost a game."

Schmittou had been at Goodlettsville High two and one-half years when his continued summer-league success began to attract the attention of some colleges that were intent on improving their baseball programs.

"I had a couple of feelers, including one from the University of Kentucky, which was interested in me as a part-time coach," says Schmittou. "But that didn't appeal to me."

Meanwhile, Jess Neely had arrived at Vanderbilt as athletic director and made it known that he was committed to improving the entire athletic department, not just the football and basketball programs.

"Vanderbilt had never had a full-time baseball coach," says Schmittou. "George Archie coached part-time and worked for the Nashville Bridge Company. The school gave no baseball scholarships.

"One of my summer-league pitchers was Elliott Jones, who threw harder than anybody who's ever been in Nashville— including Wayne Garland. His father was Dr. Ernest Jones, who taught at Vanderbilt and was on the Athletic Board.

"Dr. Jones was aware of Mr. Neely's commitment to build a better baseball program. He had become acquainted with me through his son. Again, my baseball connections played a key part in deciding which way my career would go, because it was Dr. Jones who recommended me to Mr. Neely as Vanderbilt's first full-time baseball coach.

"Of all the men I've known in my life, outside my family, Mr. Neely had the most influence on me. He called and wanted to know if I could meet him to talk about becoming the head baseball coach at Vandy as well as possibly being the head football recruiter.

"Coach Bill Pace had already interviewed some people for the football position, and when I met with Mr. Neely I said, 'I don't know if I want to be a football recruiter, and Coach Pace wants someone else, but I certainly want to coach baseball.'

"So he said, 'Come and coach baseball and between March 1 and June 1 I will pay you $1,500. And I will help you build a program. After June 1 we will find out what else you can do.'

"I don't know what it was about that man, but something about Mr. Neely made me accept this offer.

"Understand, that was a tremendous risk for me at the time. I was giving up a Metro teaching job, where I was head coach. I wasn't making much, about $9,000, but I was making another $6,000 to $7,000 at Ford, and I was making $4,000 a year being a scout for the Cleveland Indians.

"By taking the Vanderbilt baseball job, I was giving all that up. I could no longer work at Ford, I had to give up my high school coaching, and because of NCAA rules I could no longer be a professional scout.

"But something about Mr. Neely made me believe in him like I'd never believed in any person before except for my parents, so I listened to what he had to say and accepted his offer on the spot.

"It also fit my mold. I think Vanderbilt had won just two baseball games the year before, so I knew there wouldn't be any way I'd be regarded less than a success. Unlike my situation at Bailey Junior High, I was taking over a program that had only one way to go: up."

Schmittou planned to use his citywide sandlot connections and network to help him build his Vanderbilt program from scratch.

"I felt that if I could get just one scholarship, then get one-third of these guys who'd played for me in the city leagues since they were 12 years old, I could win the Southeastern Conference championship," he recalls. "And I did."

Schmittou got more than his big coaching break at Vanderbilt; he also acquired his nickname, 'Smokey.'

"It certainly didn't come from my fastball," says Schmittou. "What happened was, when I got to Vanderbilt they weren't drawing anybody for baseball so to try to get the students interested in coming out to the games, a couple of editors of the student paper, The Hustler, ran a little contest to give me a nickname. Chuck Offenburger and Doug Bates came up with the idea, and it generated a lot of interest and response. I agreed to accept whatever nickname won the contest.

"Because Walter Alston was doing so well at the time with the Dodgers, and some people called him Smokey, I guess that was a name on people's minds. That's what won the contest, and that's where I got my nickname. Smokey."

Schmittou had a baseball team and a nickname—and not much else.

"We were really starting from scratch, at rock-bottom," he says. "I got there in February, which meant that it was too late to recruit, so the team was already set. I had to take what I found.

"I knew we weren't going to be real good when Bill Brimm, the coach at Madison High, called and wanted a scrimmage game. I agreed to play, so Bill brought his high-schoolers over and beat my college guys 9–1."

Still, Schmittou was determined to squeeze the most out of what he had to work with. He came up with an "incentive plan" to make his players try harder.

"It was probably an NCAA violation," he admits, "but I made my players this offer; I promised them an extra 50 cents a day, on top of their allotted $5 meal money, for every conference game we won. We played 17 games and my guys, being the smart Vanderbilt students they were, immediately began to figure up how much money they could make.

"Well, at the end of the season they were up to $5.50 a day. We had won one conference game."

To help make ends meet, Pete Naylor, Vanderbilt's budget-conscious business manager, ordered Schmittou to sell program ads.

"Chuck Boyd, our football quarterback, and I went out and sold the heck out of those ads," says Schmittou. "We sold more ads than we knew what to do with. Finally Naylor called and said, 'Stop selling ads—the program's getting too big.'

"That never made any sense to me, but that's what he said. So we stopped selling. I guess that was the first time I noticed I had a knack for selling things."

Neely kept his promise to support the Vanderbilt baseball program, and over the next few years he secured four athletic scholarships for Schmittou.

"That was during a time when most other SEC schools had 19 baseball scholarships," says Schmittou. "We were still going up against teams that had four or five times the number of scholarships we had.

"What I'd do was take one scholarship and divide it up between three or four players."

Despite the limitations, Schmittou was eventually able to keep his promise to build Vanderbilt a championship baseball program.

During his 11 years as Commodore baseball coach, Schmittou's teams won over 300 games, four divisional titles, and two SEC championships, and Schmittou was twice named Southeastern Conference Coach of the Year.

In the process, the Schmittou legend grew. Long before Oakland Raiders owner Al Davis delivered his famous "Just win, baby, win!" credo, Schmittou was abiding by it.

If his team couldn't out-hit or out-throw or out-run an opponent, Schmittou would try his best to out-fox it.

One season Vanderbilt was playing Georgia for a berth in the SEC playoffs. Vandy won with the first game of the three-game series and was one win away from capturing the West Division title and a trip to the conference tournament.

"At the time you had to win your division to go to the play-offs," explains Schmittou, "and we were in a hot race with Georgia and Tennessee. It looked like it was going to come down to us and Georgia."

The Bulldogs arrived in Music City for the decisive showdown. The game was played at Tennessee Preparatory School, which could accommodate a larger crowd than Vandy's cramped little park. Rain was in the forecast.

Schmittou's team lost the first game of the doubleheader, but in the second game the Commodores struck early, built a lead, and held it through five innings. If they could hang on, that one win would put them in the playoffs.

"There was thunder rumbling in the distance and lightning flickering, and you could smell the rain," says Schmittou. "We knew it was going to start pouring any minute."

As the storm clouds grew darker, Georgia went to bat in the top of the sixth, and the Bulldogs began to rally. They scored two quick runs to take the lead, with no outs.

At that point Schmittou began to make a series of pitching changes.

"I was stalling for time," admits Schmittou, "because under the rules, when a game is rained out during an incomplete inning, the score reverts back to the end of the last completed inning. And if the game is through the fifth inning—as this one was—then it's an official game."

Schmittou made one pitching change. Then another. Then another.

Finally, his bullpen depleted and still no rain, Schmittou looked at his assistant, Roy Carter, and said, "Well this may be the time I have the 'suspected heart attack.'"

Instead, Schmittou instructed his final pitcher to "throw nothing but balls."

"I told him to put it over the batter's head or so far outside the strike zone nobody could touch it.

"And that's what he did. He walked the next batter. Then the next. The first man stole third, rounded the base, and came home. We let him, made no attempt to tag him out."

Suddenly Georgia's coach understood Schmittou's ploy: If Vandy didn't retire the Bulldogs before the game was rained out, the inning—and Georgia's go-ahead runs—would be wiped out.

But if Georgia could end the inning—get itself out—and retire Vandy before the game was called, the score would stand and the Dawgs would be the winners.

And so began one of the more bizarre episodes in the history of baseball.

"Their coach, realizing what we were up to, told his guys to try to get themselves out," says Schmittou, chuckling at the scenario. "They were standing between bases, trying to get themselves tagged. But my guys wouldn't do it. Then they began to step on the plate and swing at the pitch, which made them automatically out."

Finally, with Georgia trying to retire itself and Vanderbilt deliberately surrendering runs, the rain began to fall, ending the game. The score reverted back to the last complete inning, making the Commodores the winners and sending them to the SEC playoffs.

The following day Georgia informed Vanderbilt it intended to file a protest with the conference office over Schmittou's tactics, to which Schmittou caustically replied:

"Anybody who doesn't know how to make an out isn't smart enough to write a letter of protest."

The University of Georgia apparently harbored no ill will or hard feelings over Schmittou's shenanigans; in fact it apparently admired his resourcefulness because a couple of years later it tried to hire him away from Vanderbilt.

"I considered the Georgia job for about two hours," says Schmittou. "I went down to Athens for an interview with the Athletic Board, and at one point I asked about putting up lights on the baseball field.

"I was told by one board member, 'To be honest, tennis is the national championship sport here, and before we'd do that for the baseball field, we'd first light the tennis courts.'

"It took me about two hours to make up my mind: I'd be danged if I was going to play second fiddle to tennis. I was already playing second fiddle to football and basketball at Vanderbilt, and that was bad enough. I wasn't going to go to Georgia and be second fiddle to tennis.

The year after Schmittou snookered Georgia in the famous rain game, he got some home-field payback at Alabama.

"We'd won the conference in '73 and the next year they had a tournament in Tuscaloosa named after their legendary coach, Joe Sewell, who played in the majors.

"There were four teams in the tournament and we won our first game, so we were playing Alabama for the championship.

"We got on them fast and had them beat the whole ball game. We got into the bottom of the ninth and we were up two runs with two outs, two men on base. Rich Potter came up for

Alabama. We knew Potter was a good hitter so we made sure we never threw one into his strike zone. I told my pitcher to just sort of fish around, not give him anything to hit.

"We threw one outside and Potter reached out and hooked it way down the left field line. It was so far foul my leftfielder, Steve Chandler, didn't even chase it and Potter didn't even run.

"All of a sudden the umpire calls 'Fair ball!' Potter takes off and circles the bases and we lose the game on the foul ball.

"Bear Bryant, who was Alabama's athletic director at the time, came down to present the runner-up trophy in the Joe Sewell Classic and I told Bryant in no uncertain terms where he could put that trophy. It wasn't a complimentary place. Bryant just laughed; he'd watched the game and had seen what happened.

"When we went into the locker room to dress, Jim Goosetree, with the Alabama athletic department, came in with the trophy. And I promptly told Goosetree what *he* could do with it.

"We went out and got on the bus to come home, and some Alabama equipment guy came on and searched all of our players to make sure none of us had stolen any of their little red Tide towels. He didn't find any.

"A week or so after we got home, our athletic director, Clay Stapleton, came in with the trophy and said that Alabama had sent it to him and claimed I was rude to them because I wouldn't accept it.

"I promptly told Mr. Stapleton what the entire University of Alabama could do with its Joe Sewell Classic runner-up trophy. So Mr. Stapleton took it and put it in our trophy case.

"Well, we went on, had a great year, and won our division. And Alabama won its division. We're better than Alabama, we know that. But in order to win the SEC championship, we have to beat Bama two out of three.

"The first game is our place and we kill 'em; blow 'em out by about 10 runs. Then we have to go to Tuscaloosa for the next game or two if necessary.

"I've got Bob Latimer and Steve Burger ready to pitch the first game, so I know we're gonna win the SEC. Right before we leave to go to Alabama, I called our equipment manager, Bill Kelly, into my office. I asked Kelly if he could get into the trophy case and he said he could.

"I told Kelly to go get that Joe Sewell trophy and put it on the bus. We went to Alabama, played one game, and sure enough, we beat them and won the SEC championship.

"Before we left I told Kelly to steal me one of those little red Tide towels. And he did. I took that towel and wrapped it around the Joe Sewell trophy.

"On the ride home I told our bus driver to stop on the long bridge that crosses the Tennessee River near Huntsville. I said we were going to have a dedication.

"I gave my captains, Gene Menees, now with the TSSAA, and Rick Duncan, who's a preacher in Ohio, the honor of throwing that runner-up trophy, wrapped up in a red Tide towel, into the Tennessee River.

"There were two fishermen down below us, and I think they thought we were throwing a body off the bridge.

"We came on home and never told Mr. Stapleton where the Joe Sewell trophy went. As far as I know, it's still right where it belongs—on the bottom of the river."

Chapter III
Football Adventures

"It's the chase, not the kill, that makes the hunt."

While building a championship baseball program at Vanderbilt, Schmittou also became immersed in the Commodores' long-struggling football program.

"Mr. Neely said he would pay me $7,000 a year to be a football recruiter in addition to coaching baseball," says Schmittou. "Understand, that was still about one-third what I'd been making in my combined salaries before I came to Vanderbilt, but that was fine. My wife had a good job and we were paying the bills.

"So I became a Vanderbilt football recruiter, along with Bobby Cope. Bobby was about 5-foot-7, a real flashy dresser, and always smoked a big cigar.

"Bobby taught me about football recruiting. For example, he said when you're recruiting linemen, don't bother with one unless you get a crick in your neck looking up at him."

Schmittou joined the Vanderbilt football staff about the time the university began to recruit their first black athletes. Perry Wallace (one of the SEC's first black players) had been a

successful basketball player for Vanderbilt, and the football program was following that lead.

"I went to see Big John Merritt over at Tennessee State for
advice on how to go after the really good black athletes.

"I said, 'Big John, what can you tell me?'

"He said, 'Smitty, forget telling them all this bunk about
what a great job they're gonna get when they get out of college. My people don't have much money, and they want to
know what's in their immediate future. So get you a big fancy
car, some nice duds, and a big roll of money. Put a $20 bill
around a bunch of ones and put a rubber band around it. Now,
with the car, the duds, and the roll of money, you've got my
people's attention.'

"So Cope and I decided to do it. We borrowed a
Thunderbird from a friend named John Morgan. It had a TV in
it. I had only one suit, so I wore it. Cope got this big roll of
money—mostly ones, rolled inside a $20 bill, like Big John
suggested, and it looked like about $10,000. And we went off
to recruit a young gentleman from Paris, Tennessee.

"We got down there and went into the neighborhood and I
knocked on a door and asked for the kid. The man at the door
said, 'Don't know nobody by that name.'

"It occurred to me that I was a stranger in a fancy suit, and
this guy doesn't know exactly what I wanted the kid for. So I
explained that I was a college football recruiter and wanted to
take the young man to dinner and offer him a college scholarship. Taking a recruit to dinner was not an NCAA violation in
1969.

"He said, 'Oh yeah.' And he told me where I could find
the kid a couple of houses down the street. We went to eat and
Cope flashed his roll of money when it was time to pay the bill.
The young man, who was a fine student, agreed to visit
Vanderbilt and eventually signed with us."

Schmittou didn't always carry off the image of a high roller.

"A couple of weeks later I was down in Tampa," he says.

"I'd been in Florida for about two weeks recruiting, and toward the end of the trip I took a prospect and his family out to dinner at a fancy restaurant. The NCAA permitted this then.

"There were five of them and they immediately ordered a round of drinks. Then another round. Then they ordered the most expensive meals on the menu. Then they ordered dessert.

"I began to realize I had some serious trouble; I didn't know if I had enough money to pay for all that. That was back before the days of the university credit card. I always carried cash, and I knew I was running pretty low.

"I excused myself to go to the restroom. I checked my wallet to see how much money I had and found $105 and some change.

"I went back to our table and before they could order another round of drinks I explained that I had to get going because I had a long day the next morning. I quickly called for the check and when it came I saw that it totaled—and this is the honest truth—$105.

"After I paid the bill I had about 35 cents left. I didn't have anything to leave for a tip.

"I kinda eased out, knowing our waitress was glaring at me, while telling the kid and his parents that I hoped they like Vanderbilt and will keep us in mind. Of course I know the waitress was thinking, 'That cheap so-and-so didn't even leave a tip!'

"I got back to the hotel and cashed a personal check and the next morning before I left town I went by the restaurant and found our waitress. I explained what had happened the night before and gave her the tip.

"She said, 'Well, you can't imagine how I cussed you. But I sure appreciate you coming back.' The prospect signed with Florida but never played a down, so I guess we won after all."

Schmittou quickly discovered recruiting is a ruthless, no-holds-barred proposition in the football-mad Southeastern Conference.

This was 1969, and Bill Pace was our coach. I was after a recruit in Dyersburg, Tennessee, a nice kid named Danny Jefferies. He was a great player who went to Tennessee and became all-SEC.

"He committed to Vanderbilt originally. I was so happy that he was coming that I went over to the sawmill where his daddy worked. I met Mr. Jefferies and shook his hand and told him how proud I was that his son was going to play football for Vanderbilt.

"A strange look came over his face and a couple of men standing nearby looked at him kinda funny. But he didn't say anything.

"I had to get back to Nashville and coordinate everything on national signing day, so Wilford Fuqua, who was a graduate assistant, went to Dyersburg to handle Danny Jefferies' signing.

"Shortly after I got to the office that morning I got a call from Wilford, and he said he couldn't find Jefferies.

"Turns out, they had spread the word from the sawmill to some big UT supporters, including one guy who was on the board of trustees, that Jefferies had committed to Vanderbilt. So UT had swung into action. They moved in and got him, and ol' Smokey got his first hard lesson in recruiting. I, like a dummy, didn't know the rules: namely, there are no rules."

Another time, Schmittou was locked onto a recruit in Kentucky.

"We knew the competition was going to be very fierce for this young man," says Schmittou. "He came from a poor family, so we told him we could get him a job—a legitimate job—if he came to Vanderbilt.

"We said we could also make arrangements with a local car dealer to get him a car at cost and arrange financing for his father. It was such a great deal that I was sitting there thinking, 'Man, I wish I could get a deal like this myself.'

"The recruit's father was a pretty good cook, and we had checked about getting him a job at a local restaurant.

"Well, we met with the family and told them what all we'd been working on, feeling pretty good about it.

"The player and his family sat there and patiently listened to us go on for about 30 minutes. Then they began to tell us what they had in mind: the player wanted a car but had no intention of paying for one, and the father wanted to own a restaurant, not work in one.

"We walked away from that situation, and I heard later that a certain governor visited and made certain the young man stayed in Kentucky."

Schmittou attempted to recruit the great Ozzie Newsom out of Leeds, Alabama.

"Ozzie was a wonderful young man," says Schmittou. "I recruited him for two years, and he sometimes came and watched us play baseball.

"Alabama and Auburn weren't on him at first, and I thought we had him.

"About a week before the signing date I went down to check on him and I thought everything was fine. Ozzie said he planned to sign with Vanderbilt on Saturday. Next day, as I'm leaving, I happened to notice two cars parked at a little cafe in Leeds, with Alabama and Auburn stickers. I thought, 'Uh-oh.'

"I turned around and went back to check on Ozzie and he said he had changed his mind. He was going to Alabama.

"I said, 'Ozzie, you've been planning to come to Vanderbilt for two years. What changed your mind?'

"He basically said, 'You know we don't have much, and Alabama had arranged to have somebody pay me $2,000 a ticket for my four complimentary game tickets.' Ticket scalping was legal in Alabama and a player's selling his complimentary tickets was not an NCAA violation at the time.

"I said, 'Ozzie, I don't blame you,' and I came on home.

"I went in and told Steve Sloan, our head coach at the time, what had happened—that Alabama had made Ozzie an offer he couldn't refuse.

"Sloan slapped his fist on the table and said, 'Dang! Johnny Musso (their All-American running back) only got $1,000 a ticket!'"

Schmittou quickly learned to play the game.

"There was a great player at White County High in Sparta, Tennessee, named David Culley," he says, "and we wanted him at Vanderbilt.

"Coach Gene Windham had been on Culley hard and we thought we had him. Windham went to Sparta to meet with David after a basketball game one night and I went with him. We got to Shoney's and David walked in—surrounded by Sparta's football coaches, who were all big UT people. Right off I knew what was happening: another Dyersburg!

"So Gene and I left and went on over to Culley's house and waited for him with his father. Mr. Culley called and told the coaches to bring David home. And they did. They agreed to bring David to his own house.

"When he arrived, I asked David, 'Do you want to go to UT?'

"He glanced at the coaches and said, 'Yes.'

"We all stood around awhile talking, and as Windham and I were leaving, I whispered to David again, 'Do you really want to go to UT?'

"And this time he said 'No.'

"I whispered, 'Just hang loose.'

"Gene and I waited outside until the coaches left, then we went back in and told David we'd pick him up in the morning and take him to Nashville. But we made a mistake—as soon as we left, the coaches came back. They'd been waiting for us to leave.

"We went back to the motel and Windham was beside himself. He was crying, 'We've lost Culley! We've lost him!'

"And I said, 'Not yet.' I called three of our players at Vanderbilt—Joe Reynolds, Doug Nettles, and Walter Overton. I said, 'I need you guys in Sparta. We're about to lose Culley.

I need some help.'

"In an hour and a half they rolled up with their girlfriends, all charged up, ready to help us get Culley.

"I said, 'If you do find him, make sure nobody else finds him, and have him at McGugin Center tomorrow at noon.'

"And they did. I don't know where or how they found him, but they had him at Vanderbilt the next day, and we signed him.

"UT heard about it, of course, and they were ill. Mr. (Bill) Johnson, a former great UT player and a banker in Sparta who is also on the UT Board of Trustees, about had a fit over it. But we won that battle."

When Sloan replaced Pace as Vanderbilt football coach, he didn't want to keep Schmittou as head recruiter, "even though I'd become pretty good at it.

"But Sloan wanted to bring in his own man, Mike Pope, from Florida State. Sloan wanted me to stay on as an assistant recruiter. I wasn't about to be anybody's assistant, but I stayed as head recruiter.

"Sloan brought in one of the finest staffs you'll ever see. He had a perfect complement of people: Rex Dockery, Mr. Optimistic. Always had a smile on his face and made you feel good. And Bill Parcells: Mr. Tough. Parcells was our defensive coordinator and linebacker coach.

"I immediately became good friends with Parcells. He was a great motivator and loved baseball.

"When we'd have a staff meeting to discuss recruiting, we'd go 'round the table and tell Sloan, a fine Christian man, who we were looking at.

"It was always 'Bob so-and-so, 6-4, 210, a member of the Fellowship of Christian Athletes . . .' Everybody tried to impress Sloan with what fine young men they were recruiting.

"One day we're going around the table like that and Parcells, who always sat next to me, leaned over and whispered, 'Schmittou, while you're recruiting all them Fellowship of Christian Athletes, how about recruiting me a thug or two? I'll take one of them also.'

"Parcells had nothing against the FCA, understand, but he was tough. And he liked tough players. He might not get the best athletes, but he got the toughest kids.

"I'll give you one perfect example: Damon Regen. He was not heavily recruited out of high school, and by SEC linebacker standards he was too small to be a good prospect. Too short. But he was tough as nails. He was Parcells' kind of player.

"Those were the kind of players Parcells liked: The Damon Regens, the Tate Riches, the Tom Galbierzes. They were tough and they could play within a system.

"As a recruiter, I learned that sometimes the best players aren't the ones who jump right out at you. You've got to look at the inside as much as the outside."

It seemed that the better Schmittou became at college recruiting, the more he came to detest it.

He discovered that everybody bent the rules, including Vanderbilt.

"There wasn't a single big-time football school anywhere who didn't fudge a little," he says. "I imagine it still goes on today. I know for a fact it did back when I was in the middle of recruiting, because I witnessed it first-hand."

Schmittou insists that Vanderbilt, with its reputation for academic excellence, strived to maintain equal integrity in its athletic department. But as he says, nobody was snow-white. Not even Vandy.

One of Schmittou's Commodore coaching associates once loaned a recruit his telephone credit card—a blatant violation of NCAA rules—and it was discovered by, of all schools, Vandy's arch rival, Tennessee.

Schmittou picks up the story:

"One day our business manager got a phone bill for about $9,000, all charged to one credit card. Our AD called me up and said, 'Is your card number so-and-so?'

"I said no, that wasn't my card number.

"Well, our AD keeps calling and checking until he finds the coach that card was issued to. He called the coach in and we found out what happened: He had loaned the card to a recruit, and Tennessee found out about it. UT's coaches got the card from the kid and used it for a month to make their recruiting calls.

"Of course Tennessee knows we'll find out what they've done when the bill comes due. But they also know that Vanderbilt can't do a thing about it. What our guy did was a clear violation of NCAA rules so we can't turn UT in without admitting we broke the rules ourselves. I could just imagine the Tennessee coaches sitting around laughing about it.

"Eventually I think the two head coaches (Vandy's Fred Pancoast and Tennessee's Bill Battle) got together, talked the situation over, and decided just to forget about it. As far as I know, that's where it ended."

Not all the recruiting shenanigans were so benign and humorous, and eventually they began to weigh on Schmittou's conscience.

"To be a successful recruiter you had to do what the competition did," he says. "And more and more, I was becoming uncomfortable with what I was being forced to do to compete with other schools for top prospects. I got to where I didn't like looking in the mirror after a recruiting trip."

Schmittou's reprieve came in 1975, when the NCAA passed a rule eliminating all schools' full-time recruiters on the road.

"That axed one of my jobs at Vanderbilt and immediately cut my pay from $20,000 to $14,000 a year," says Schmittou. "But to be honest, at that point I didn't care. I was relieved to be out of it. I'd had my fill of college football recruiting.

"The only problem I had was the way they went about it. One day Mr. Clay Stapleton, our athletic director, called me into his office and announced that my position in football had been eliminated. Ken Hudgens, who was my assistant, was transferred to another position in the athletic department and I was now just the head baseball coach—making $6,000 a year less.

"I thought I deserved better than that. I had contributed a lot to the school, both as baseball coach and football recruiter. Most schools around the country, faced with the same cutback, simply moved their recruiters into other positions, but I wasn't given that option.

"The day it happened I was asked by Nashville *Tennessean* sports writer Jimmy Davy if I was going to remain at Vanderbilt. I kinda bit my tongue, because I didn't need to be criticizing anybody. But I'd made up my mind that I was getting out.

"Actually, even before they cut my job and my pay, I had pretty much made up my mind to get into something else in the next four or five years. After Mr. Neely left as AD, the support for baseball just wasn't there.

"One year I needed one more scholarship to put together a great team—a team that could take the next step and go on from SEC contender to national contender. But Vanderbilt wouldn't give me that one extra scholarship. Consequently, I lost Rick Honeycutt—who wanted to play for Vandy—to Tennessee. Honeycutt could've made us a contender for the national championship.

"My baseball operating budget never went up from the time Mr. Neely left in 1972 to the time I left in 1979. It was $12,000, compared with $50,000 or $60,000 for some of the top schools. My recruiting budget stayed at $500. I had to rely on my pro scouting connections for most of my recruiting. You couldn't do much traveling on $500.

"So that's why I didn't say much when they took away my football position. I had made up my mind that I had gone about as far at Vanderbilt as I could go, given the limitations and restrictions I had to work under.

"Despite all that, they still did me a favor getting me out of football recruiting. It was the most distasteful job I've ever had in my life. My whole career depended on some 17-year-old kid. And if you played completely by the rules, you knew you might as well write off certain top players.

"As I said, Vanderbilt for the most part tried to stay within the rules, so it was really frustrating to have to sit back and lose a good kid to some other school that wasn't playing by the same rules. You'd work so hard for a kid, then learn that it was going to take more than a scholarship to get him.

"Also, the rules were so complicated. As a recruiter you were limited to a certain number of contacts with a player. But let's say I ran into Mike Wright, whom I had known for years, when he was being recruited. I would say hello to him and technically that was a rules violation.

"The alumni could also be a problem. You had to get them involved, writing letters and so on, but you were always scared that someone would do something they weren't supposed to do. How are you supposed to control that? You can't watch over every single alum or booster, and that's where a lot of recruiting violations take place.

"I also didn't like to put pressure on the kids. I was uncomfortable with the high-pressure sales. The process wasn't fair to them—being pulled this way and that by a bunch of adults, with a lot of different people promising them different things.

"It was like being an encyclopedia salesman—get in, make the sale, get out. Only we weren't selling encyclopedias, we were grown men trying to lure a kid to a certain school.

"Now I admit I was good at it—my last year with Pancoast we had one of the top-rated recruiting classes in the nation. We brought in some great athletes. But I wasn't sorry to get out of the business.

"This was in the mid-1970s and maybe things have changed since then. I sure hope so, but I kinda doubt it. In fact, judging from the things I still hear and read about, the situation may be worse than ever. I'm just glad I'm no longer a part of it."

During his days on the Vanderbilt football staff, Schmittou had some fun with Pete Naylor, the department business manager who had a reputation for running a tight ship.

"Once I went on a recruiting trip in Kentucky and turned in a couple of toll-booth charges on my expense account," says Schmittou. "It wasn't much—a couple of dollars—but Naylor wouldn't pay it because I didn't bring back a receipt. I didn't care about the money; it was the principle of the thing.

"So I got him back one football season. Morganna, who became famous as baseball's Kissing Bandit, was dancing at a club in Printer's Alley that fall. The club owner called my office one day and said Morganna wanted to go to a football game, so I left her a ticket at the gate. And the seat was right smack in the middle of the section where the coaches' wives sat.

"Morganna showed up wearing an outfit that might have gotten her arrested and went up and sat down in the seat I'd got for her. Everybody in the section was staring at her, wondering who she was and how she'd got there.

"Next day Naylor came charging into the football office, demanding to know who put a stripper in the coaches' wives section. I never confessed."

Schmittou's best friend on the Vandy staff was Bill Parcells, the hard-nosed defensive coordinator.

"I called him 'Puma' because I never saw him wearing anything but Puma tennis shoes," says Schmittou. "I used to accuse him of wearing them to church.

"He used to come over to my office and sit around and talk baseball. He grew up in New York and hung out at the old Polo Grounds. Today he can still probably name the entire starting lineups for the 1953 Dodgers, Giants, and Yankees.

"We used to play a game called 20 Questions, where you try to guess a sports personality by asking questions and getting clues. Parcells was excellent at it, whether it was football, baseball, or any other sport. He knew 'em all.

"He also liked to play gin rummy, and we got a game up and kept it going for years. I accused Parcells of finally leaving town because he got so far behind. Actually, he's a little ahead, but whenever he stops winning Super Bowls I plan to even it up.

"We'd go to baseball games together and he was simply terrible. We'd go to high school games, college games, whatever. He drove me crazy because I'd want to talk to the coaches and Puma would want to sit off somewhere by himself. He'd be yelling at me to come on, hurry up, and I'd be trying to carry on a conversation.

"Every time we'd play a home game Parcells would drop by our dugout, poke his head in, and holler, 'Schmittou, can't you find anybody to get anybody out?' Then he'd take off before I could answer.

"One day we were playing Georgia and we were struggling. Parcells was on his way to spring practice and stuck his head in and said, 'Schmittou, can't you get anybody out?'

"Well, I wasn't in a good mood right then, so I told Puma to go to hell. He laughed and went on his way.

"After our game was over, I went over to the football field where they were having a scrimmage. Parcells' defense was getting whipped all over the field by the offense. The offense was just marching up and down the field. And of course Parcells is fussing and cussing and yelling at everybody.

"After it's over, the defense comes trudging by, and all their heads are hanging, and I yell, 'Hey, Big Puma! When the heck are you going to get somebody who can tackle somebody?'

"Parcells let out a roar and came after me. Chased me down the street in front of the stadium. I told him he could dish it out but he couldn't take it.

"Parcells wasn't faking his temper. He was really that temperamental and fiery. One game we had a big old defensive tackle who was getting whipped bad, and finally Parcells called him over to the sideline.

"He said, 'Look, I'm going to give you two choices: You can get back out on that field and whip that son of a gun across the line from you, or else you're gonna have to whip my butt right here and now, in front of all these people.' And he was dead serious. The big lineman jogged back out and played a heck of a game the rest of the way. He was afraid not to."

Schmittou could always appreciate the humor in a situation.

"One time I walked into the lockerroom and Parcells and some of the other coaches were standing around Tom Galbierz, one of our big linemen, and he was swallowing salt tablets.

"Then he got a tongue depressor and shoved it down his throat. Then Bill Kelly, our equipment manager, produced a fifth of whiskey from somewhere and Galbierz took a big swallow.

"I watched all this for a minute, then I said, 'Galbierz, what's your problem?'

"And he says, 'Coach, I was eating supper awhile ago and I swallowed my gold tooth. I paid $100 for that tooth and I'm trying to vomit it up.'

"I said, 'If you really want to vomit, go up to my office, open my desk drawer, and get out a package of Red Man chewing tobacco I keep in there. Get yourself a big chaw, work it up real good, and swallow it.'

"He did, and a few minutes later, he was vomiting all over the place. And he got his gold tooth back."

When Steve Sloan departed Vanderbilt, Parcells could have had the head coaching job.

"They interviewed Richard Williamson, John Cooper, Fred Pancoast, and Parcells," recalls Schmittou. "When it came time for Parcells' interview, he called me and asked me to meet him at a local restaurant to talk about it.

"He said, 'What do you think they're gonna ask me?'

"I told him probably just the usual things, about where he thought he could take the program.

"He went in for the interview about 4 in the afternoon.

About 8 that night he called me at home and said, 'The job's mine if I want it. But I'm not going to take it.'

"I asked why not.

"He said, 'Because I can't be successful here. I can't win at Vanderbilt the way things are.'

"He didn't think he could work for Clay Stapleton. He didn't think the commitment was there for football, just as I knew it wasn't there for baseball. I told him I thought he'd probably made a wise decision."

Parcells left Vanderbilt, knocked around in the college ranks at different schools, and eventually emerged as head coach of the NFL's New York Giants. He went on to coach the Giants to two Super Bowl championships and gained a national reputation as one of the finest minds and motivators in all of football.

"Vanderbilt could have had him," says Schmittou. "I've often wondered what would have happened if they had made Parcells head coach and given him the support to build a program.

"I don't think Vanderbilt football would have ever been the same."

That's not a criticism of Pancoast or any of the other Vanderbilt football coaches who have struggled over the years to field a winning team in what is generally considered the nation's toughest football conference.

"They're good people, good coaches, and all of them worked hard," Schmittou says. "Fred Pancoast is a perfect example. He came to Vanderbilt with excellent credentials, and he worked as hard as anybody can work. I know how disappointing and frustrating it was for him. It's just a very tough job. Fred is a good man and good friend and I wish he could have succeeded—just as I wish one of my former football and baseball players, Watson Brown, could have succeeded.

"I still have very fond feelings for Vanderbilt and its athletic programs. Nobody would like to see them succeed more than me. But in football, it's awfully hard. That's just the reality of the situation."

CHAPTER IV
SOUNDS OF SUCCESS

"If you prepare yourself,
perhaps your chance will come."

While Vanderbilt athletic director Jess Neely exerted tremendous influence on Larry Schmittou's career, Neely's successor, Clay Stapleton, represented an equal force—but in the opposite direction.

Stapleton's refusal to give Schmittou another job in the athletic department after phasing out his football recruiting duties—and related salary—would drive Schmittou from the coaching ranks.

"Losing half my job and half my pay forced me to sit down and make some decisions," says Schmittou. "I had a wife (Shirley, his high school sweetheart) and five kids. I had a growing family, and I decided I couldn't make enough coaching baseball to support it."

Schmittou began to dabble in various sidelines.

"I tried working as a night auditor at a local motel, and there I met a friend, Jim Folkes, and he and I formed our own tour company. I got involved mainly because I wanted to take my baseball team to Hawaii, and we ended up selling out an entire 747. That was my first taste of promotion."

Schmittou also got involved in real estate, delving into the home-building industry.

"My bankers let me have some money to get started and my partner and I began building houses. We built some great houses, but there was just one problem: nobody bought them.

"We got into the business just when the bottom dropped out of the market. Before we knew what we were doing, we'd lost a tidy sum. All the while, the interest on our original loan kept mounting. We got to where we owed about $80,000 and the bank informed me in no uncertain terms that I was responsible for paying it all back.

"So after a couple of years of dabbling in other businesses I knew absolutely nothing about, I found myself still not making enough to live on at Vanderbilt—plus in debt to the bank for $80,000. I sat down and decided I wasn't getting very far.

"I reached an important decision. The only thing I really knew much about was baseball. If I was going to make a living, it would have to be in baseball."

And so out of financial desperation began the first flickerings of a dream to bring professional baseball to Nashville.

"About that time, in 1977, Chattanooga bought Birmingham's Class AA team. Bear Bryant's son had been general manager in Birmingham and the team was drawing nobody. So Birmingham sold out to Chattanooga.

"Chattanooga had been without a pro team for several years, kinda like Nashville had been after the old Nashville Vols folded. I thought the two situations were similar in Nashville and Chattanooga. I was curious to see how the new minor-league team would do in Chattanooga.

"I was down there looking at a prospect for Vanderbilt, and the Lookouts were playing a night game. I went over to

Engel Stadium and discovered they had a sellout, about 7,000 people.

"I talked to the owner, Walter Reed, and he said he didn't pay much for the team. he said he got it from Birmingham because they were basically broke.

"I thought to myself, 'If Chattanooga can draw like this with hardly any work or promotion, think what a team could do if somebody really worked at it.' "

The dream was born.

"I had some pretty good major-league connections through my college coaching and pro scouting, so when I got home I began to make some phone calls," says Schmittou.

"I was told by more than one club that if I could provide a suitable park they would be willing to put a minor-league team in Nashville. So all I needed was a ball park."

Schmittou made his first pitch to the Metro Board of Parks and Recreation.

"I said if they'd build a municipal ball park, I could bring a professional team to town," says Schmittou. "I figured they'd jump at the proposal.

"Instead, Charlie Spears, who was superintendent of the Park Board, looked me right in the eye and said, 'I can assure you right now that neither the Park Board nor the city of Nashville is going to put one penny up to build a baseball stadium.'

"I was stunned. And crushed. I couldn't believe a city the size of Nashville had absolutely no interest in building a baseball stadium that would bring a pro team to town. I couldn't believe they just blew me off like that."

Spears didn't completely slam the door in Schmittou's face. He left it cracked just a bit.

"He told me that the city was building a new softball complex at Cedar Hill and closing the old one at Fort Negley. He said the Park Board might be willing to lease the Fort Negley site if I would build a stadium on it.

"There was just one drawback to that idea: I didn't have any money."

Schmittou left the meeting dejected but not defeated.

"I never quit thinking about it," he says. "Every time my Vanderbilt baseball team went on the road, if the town had a stadium I'd make a point to go check it out.

"For instance, we played a tournament in Oxford, Mississippi, one spring and I drove on down to Jackson to look at their ballpark. I talked to the owner, I talked to the groundskeepers. How you doing? How much you taking in? How much are your operating expenses?

Schmittou's stadium research was not always reassuring.

"I went to Evansville, Indiana, and they were really struggling," he says. "Then I went to Knoxville where we were playing UT and they weren't drawing anybody for minor-league games. It was the old-timey, just open-up-the-park kind of operation. No promotions, no nothing.

"I went to the office of the guy who owned the team. He also owned a dry-cleaning company. He said he made his money before the season ever started. He paid the city $1 a year in rent, and the city cleaned up the stadium, took care of the grounds, and paid the light bill. He couldn't lose.

"The team's parent club, the Chicago White Sox, was really struggling at the time. They actually paid an extra $40,000 for the privilege of putting a team in Knoxville. The team was drawing only about 400 to 500 a game and cutting corners to the bone.

"They would pay kids to stand behind the stands and catch fly balls. The kids could return the balls for 50 cents each. The balls were then washed off and sent back down to the field to be used again. In other words, they weren't spending a penny on the team."

Schmittou didn't think that was any way to run a ball club. He saved his visit to Columbus, Ohio, for last. They had revived AAA baseball after a long absence, and George Sisler, brother of former Nashville Vols manager Dick Sisler, had made them a tremendous success. George and one of his associates,

Dick Fitzpatrick, were tremendously helpful to Schmittou.

"I remain thankful for their help," he says.

They convinced Schmittou that a good team, in a good stadium, would do well in Nashville with good management. But how to go about it? He couldn't get a team without a stadium, and he couldn't get a stadium without money.

"I was back to square one," says Schmittou. "Broke. Then it occurred to me that even though I didn't have any money, I knew people who did. I wondered if they might be interested in helping get a stadium."

Schmittou quietly began to search for Nashvillians who shared his love of the game and who might be able to lend a hand, financially, to his minor-league plan.

"All this was happening in the summer of 1977," says Schmittou. "I was coaching a Vanderbilt baseball camp at the time and one of the players who came out was a good-looking kid who had some ability in left field. Turned out he was the son of Conway Twitty, who was a top country star. I'd noticed Conway at some of our games and practices, hanging out around the fence by himself.

"About the same time, one of the Nashville newspapers got hold of a rough sketch I'd made of a baseball stadium and ran it along with a story about me wanted to someday bring a team to town.

"The next day, Snuffy Miller, a friend of mine, called and said Conway Twitty wanted to see me. Conway had seen the story in the paper and was interested in what I had in mind.

"Understand, I'd never met Conway; my only connection with him was having seen him watching his son Jimmy play in some of our games. Until he told Snuffy to get in touch with me, I didn't know Conway even knew I existed."

Schmittou quickly agreed to set up a meeting with Twitty. The next day they got together and began to talk baseball.

"I explained what I had in mind," says Schmittou. "I wanted to build a stadium, bring in a team, and form a limited partnership.

"Conway listened for awhile and said he liked the idea. He said to count him in. We stood up and shook hands, and I guess if there was a single moment when I felt I was actually going to be able to pull this thing off, that was it. Conway gave me hope that it could be done."

Twitty, at the time an international recording star, had been in love with baseball all his life. In fact, during his youth, Twitty had been an excellent player in Arkansas; many felt he'd had big-league potential. But about the time his baseball skills were developing, he fell under the influence of a singer named Elvis and decided to seek his fortune on the stage rather than on the diamond.

But his affection for the game had not waned. He shared Schmittou's vision of bringing baseball to Music City.

"I left that meeting with Conway feeling that we were really on our way," says Schmittou. "Then he called me the next morning and said he had run the idea of investing in a ball team through his financial people and they didn't share his enthusiasm.

"He said Roy Clark had gotten involved with a team in Tulsa and he and the other investors had lost a bunch of money. He said his people advised against it.

"My heart sank.

"But then Conway went on. He said he had intended to buy 90 percent of my team and despite his financial people's advice he was still going to buy 20 percent, and he said if I couldn't find investors, he would go ahead and put the rest of it up because he'd told me he would.

"Conway said he'd work on some other investors. He said he would use his country music connections, and that's how Cal Smith and a lot of the other stars became involved. Conway brought them in."

Schmittou recalls Twitty's recruitment of Smith:

"I was sitting in Conway's office and he picked up the

phone and called Cal. He said for him and his wife to come over a minute—and bring their checkbook. They came in and Conway introduced us. He told them I was the guy who was going to bring professional baseball back to Nashville and that I was looking for investors.

"He told Cal to write me a check, and he did, right there on the spot, no questions asked. Now we had Conway Twitty and Cal Smith. And we were on our way."

Schmittou's list of investors began to grow: L. E. White, Farrell Owens, Reese Smith Jr., Billy Griggs, Bob Elliott, Gene Smith, Walter Nipper. . . .

"I knew who in Nashville loved baseball," says Schmittou. "Most of them were acquaintances or close friends. Some of them were like me—they had no money. But some of them were in good shape financially and were willing to get involved.

"Mr. Nipper, for example, was one of the most highly respected businessmen in our community. He ran a sporting goods store and I had gotten to know him over the years, buying equipment from him for my ball teams. When Mr. Nipper said to put him down for 10 percent of our team, that immediately gave us a lot of credibility from a business standpoint."

One of the earliest investors, after Conway Twitty and Cal Smith, was another popular entertainer, Jerry Reed. Reed had gained a reputation not only as one of Nashville's hottest pickers and singers but also as a movie star in such films as *W.W. and the Dixie Dance Kings*, and later in the *Smokey and the Bandit* movies with Burt Reynolds.

Reed was also a diehard Vanderbilt fan.

"Jerry would entertain our recruits, always do whatever we asked of him at Vanderbilt," says Schmittou. "That's how I got to know him.

"One day he was attending a football practice, and I noticed him leaning up against a coaches tower. I walked over and said, 'Jerry, I've got something I want you to look at.'

"He said, 'What is it, Smokey?'

"I told him I was going to bring professional baseball back to Nashville, and I wanted him to buy at least one unit, 5 percent, of ownership.

"He said, 'How much does it cost?'

"I told him, and he said 'OK, I'll buy it. Don't bother me with the details.'

"That was the quickest sale I ever made."

While Schmittou was beating the bushes for investors, he was at the same time negotiating a lease agreement with the city of Nashville for the Fort Negley property.

"I had been told by the Parks Board that I could lease the old Fort Negley property if I wanted it," says Schmittou, "because the city was moving its softball complex to a new field.

"Frankly, I didn't like the location. Even back then I could see it didn't have enough room for parking. I asked about a site in Shelby Park or Centennial Park, where the Sportsplex is now. I was told those locations were off-limits.

"So I really had only one option: accept the Fort Negley site or forget the whole thing. That was the only option the Park Board gave me. Take it or leave it. So I took it.

"I went ahead and commissioned an architect to put together a tentative stadium plan. I had a friend, Jim Reed, with the firm Stoll-Reed, and I explained to him what I wanted. The big question I had was how much was it going to cost?

"Jim said he thought I could build a stadium for $400,000 to $500,000. I figured I could handle that.

"Understand, I'm proceeding with all this under the assumption that I've got the lease all wrapped up. The Park Board had voted unanimously to grant me a 20-year lease, the terms being that in the first 10 years I agreed to build a stadium costing at least $400,000 and seating 6,500. The second 10 years I would pay the city 7 percent of our total revenue. I thought that seemed simple and clear.

"Then I got my first lesson in Nashville politics.

"This was completely new territory for me. I'd never been

involved or interested in politics. I was just a baseball coach who wanted to bring a ball team to town.

"Looking back, I was really naive. Getting involved in local politics would prove to be the most frustrating thing in my life.

"I had assumed that since the Park Board had agreed to let me lease the property—which was just sitting there, growing weeds—that was all there was to it.

"I wasn't asking for any money, but I was told the deal still had to be approved by the Metro Budget and Finance Committee. I went down to appear before the Committee and I was about to get an education in how things work in this town.

"One councilman, Carney Patterson, interrogated me as if I were on trial. He acted like I was doing something wrong. I almost said right then, 'Screw this!'

"They were afraid I was going to go broke. Was I going to guarantee this? Am I going to guarantee that? All the thoughts on that committee were that I was going to go broke, that baseball would not work in this city. They seemed to think, 'This man is going to open a park, operate awhile, and we're going to be stuck with the stadium.'

"I was completely taken aback. I'm thinking, 'What is this?' I was totally unprepared for such a hostile reception. I was getting the financing, building the stadium, and taking 100 percent of the risk. The city couldn't lose. The worst that could happen would be—even if my investors and I went broke—the city would have a new stadium built on what was then a vacant lot.

"Finally a couple of other councilmen, Elsie Jones and Buster Boguskie, got up and said some good things, and we were able to get the proposal to the Council floor. But the fight still wasn't over.

"One Council member was against it because the stadium wasn't in his district, where old Sulphur Dell had been. Another councilman, Tandy Wilson, was going around wearing a UT sweater, saying 'Are we going to build Vanderbilt a stadium?' He didn't like it because I was coaching at Vanderbilt.

"Then there was a beer controversy. Were we going to sell beer in the stadium? Yes, we were. Some councilmen were upset over that.

"It was one thing after another. The whole tone of the meeting was negative. I couldn't believe what I was hearing.

"The mayor (Richard Fulton) really took no part in it. He didn't seem to want to get involved. He neither helped us nor hurt us.

"When it was finally said and done, we had 30 votes for the stadium and 10 against it. The 30 who voted yes really didn't seem all that enthusiastic. But at least we had made it through. Within two years the ones who were afraid we would go broke were complaining that we were making too much money.

"We got past that hurdle, but not before I had gotten a good lesson in how things operated in Nashville. It had been a struggle and I got the feeling it wasn't going to be the last battle I have to fight with our local politicians.

"They disgusted me then and they disgust me even more today."

All the while he was trying to sell the stadium idea to the Metro Council, Schmittou was attempting to sell tickets to the public to watch a team that had yet to be named play in a park that had yet to be built. It wasn't an easy sell.

"I had raised about $300,000 through investors, including $30,000 I borrowed to buy my 10 percent ownership," says Schmittou. "Each 5 percent share was worth $15,000, and I felt we were in good shape.

"But the stadium was projected to cost at least $400,000 so I was still $100,000 short.

"I decided to start a ticket drive to raise the rest of the money. That way I'd have no debt. Keep in mind, my net worth at the time was below zero. I still owed the bank about $80,000 I'd lost in my home-building career, plus the $30,000 I had borrowed for my share of the ball club.

"I had a wife, five kids, and a six-year-old car and had just taken a major pay cut at Vanderbilt. So I knew a banker wasn't going to run out and hug me if I came in and asked to borrow $100,000.

"So the ticket drive was going to be critical as a means of coming up with the rest of the money I had to have."

Schmittou began to spread the word through his network of baseball buddies and the Nashville media.

"I sent a letter to 100 people I knew in baseball, people I had worked with at Ford, people I knew around town. I started it off, 'I need your help.'

"Out of the 100 people I wrote, I think 98 showed up for a meeting at McGugin Center the next week. I explained what I wanted: for each of them to sell 10 season tickets at $200 each.

"Some people were saying, 'Larry, this won't work.' These were people who were my friends, and we were talking frankly, the way you'd talk among friends.

"Amazingly, a few other people showed up, guys like John Sloan who was president of First Tennessee Bank, and I thought that was a good sign.

"I forget who the first person was who stood up and said, 'I'll help you,' but I do remember some people like John A. McPherson, the best referee in the SEC and a former minor-league player, who said, 'I ain't going to sell 10 tickets. I'm going to sell 50.'

"Jack Lavender, who I'd worked with at Ford, said he'd take a pledge card. Joe Carr, former Secretary of State, said he would help. And it took off from there.

"After we finished, we walked outside and there was seven inches of snow on the ground. Everybody laughed. There we were, planning to sell baseball tickets to a team we didn't have yet, in the middle of a snowstorm."

The advance ticket drive didn't always go so smoothly. Schmittou once brought Ernie Banks and Phil Niekro into town for a ticket promotion at Hillsboro High School.

"The theme was how everybody in Nashville could get involved with our effort," says Schmittou. "I figured with guys like Ernie Banks and Phil Niekro we'd have a great turnout.

"I drove over that night, all excited, and walked into the room where we were holding the meeting. There were 10 people sitting there. Talk about feeling embarrassed...and devastated.

"But Banks and Niekro never let on. They did a great job, telling everybody to get behind the project. They talked baseball and signed free autographs—that didn't take long—and then the meeting broke up.

"As we were leaving, a guy came over and introduced himself as Bill Dinkler. He said he worked for Budweiser and told me if I'd come to see him he'd buy some of everything we had. So I left the meeting with a good feeling. It wasn't a wasted night."

Still, Schmittou began to sense that selling tickets might be a tougher task than he had imagined. He had another idea.

"Farrell Owens and I had been talking about how many hundreds of people played softball and baseball in the city," says Schmittou. "So we came up with this plan to see if we could get them to buy a $10 coupon good for 10 general admission tickets.

"We got the order forms printed up with prepaid postage— we wanted to make it as easy to order as possible—and we went around to all the city parks and distributed them. After a couple of weeks I went down to the post office to check the box and there were about 500 of the forms stuffed in there. I thought, 'Oh, boy. People are responding.'

"But when I started opening them up I found that only about half a dozen contained checks. The other 495 or so were empty. People had mailed them back in out of meanness. And we had to pay the postage.

"The late Lon Varnell, a veteran promoter who had booked everybody from Liberace to Lawrence Welk to Barbara Mandrell, once told me Nashville was the toughest place in

America to sell tickets. I was starting to believe him. But it was too late to back out now."

With a lease secured, a stadium in the works, and a ticket sale under way, there was just one more little detail Schmittou had to attend to: He needed a team.

"For the past year or so I had been checking around the major leagues, getting a feel for what minor-league teams might be available," he says. "Farrell and I decided to attend the 1976 Baseball Winter Meeting in Los Angeles and try to meet some of the owners and executives first-hand.

"It was an experience. I arrived with about $100 in my pocket and Farrell had maybe $150. We checked into the hotel, sharing a room, and started trying to figure out what we needed to do. We quickly discovered that baseball is a tight, close-knit fraternity, and we were strictly outsiders. We couldn't get into any of the meetings. We had to sit outside in the hall and try to meet people when they came out."

Owens remembers it well:

"You talk about a couple of country bumpkins. Larry and I each owned one suit, which we wore for four days running. If we'd been the same size we could have swapped them back and forth.

"We lived on McDonald's for four days and listened to the speeches from outside the banquet rooms."

Schmittou and Owens used a pencil and hotel stationery to write letters of introduction to each of the 26 team farm directors attending the meeting and had the letters sent to their rooms.

"We explained that we were there to explore getting a minor-league team for Nashville," says Schmittou. "We put down our room number and waited to hear from someone. We waited. And waited. And waited. Nobody called."

One night as Schmittou and Owens were stalking the lobby, Charlie Finley, the colorful owner of the Oakland A's, came through, bouncing a ball off the walls.

"Then the president of the American Association, who had terrible eyesight, came by and we started talking to him," says Schmittou. "Someone walked by and said, 'Hello, Joe,' and kept going.

"Our guy turned around and talked 30 minutes to a potted plant. Farrell and I just sat there, watching Charlie Finley bounce his ball off the wall and waiting for our man to finish his conversation with the plant.

"Another night we attended a seminar on how to sell baseball on the radio. It was a great seminar; unfortunately, we never got to follow up on it because the guy who was giving it died in his room that night."

Finally, on the third day of the meeting, Schmittou's phone rang. It was Chief Bender of the Cincinnati Reds. He had received Schmittou's letter and he was interested in talking. He asked Schmittou if he could come up to his suite.

"We didn't have a suite; we had the worst room in the hotel," says Schmittou. "We told Bender we'd meet him in the lobby. Then we went on back where Avis had a car rental office set up and we asked the guy behind the booth if we could borrow his office for a few minutes. He said sure, so Farrell and I took Chief Bender inside the Avis office and presented our plan.

"Basically, Bender said, 'You build a stadium and we'll put a team in Nashville.' "

Schmittou and Farrell returned home elated. But that elation didn't last long.

"It was time to start checking the bids for the stadium and we all gathered to see what we had," says Schmittou.

"Remember, we were expecting something between $400,000 and $500,000. The first bid was opened and it was for $1.2 million. I gasped and didn't stop gasping as bid after bid was opened.

"When the last bid had been opened, the lowest one on the table was for $980,000—almost twice the highest figure we had anticipated."

Little Larry Schmittou as an infant (left), as a toddler on his family's farm (right), and with his older sister, Gladys (below right).

Left: Schmittou walks hand-in-hand down Church Street with his mother, Jane Ann. She also walked with her son to his first baseball games at old Sulphur Dell.

Above right: Schmittou visits with his future mother-in-law, Rachel Reynolds. Left: Later he and wife-to-be, Shirley, get all dressed up for a date as college freshmen.

Nashville Vols manager Larry Gilbert (on left), for whom Schmittou was named, visits with the opposing manager before Opening Day 1942.

Schmittou (back row) with, from left, brother Leo, mother Jane Ann, father Egbert, sister Gladys, and brother Harry. His other brother, John, snapped the photo of his parents' 50th wedding anniversary.

A youthful Schmittou, still in high school, with his 1957 Little League squad.

Schmittou referees a Gary-Y football game, one of the ways he earned money for college.

Schmittou (center) with two of his 1964 American Legion players, Dave Jessup and Sonny Rogers. Jessup died in Vietnam, where a field is named in his honor, and Rogers in now an executive with a Nashville construction firm.

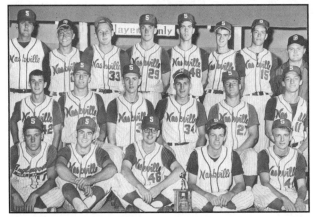

Schmittou with the team he coached to the 1965 Connie Mack World Series. Players include future major league star Sam Ewing (No. 29); Roy Carter (second from left, middle row), who became a Vanderbilt assistant and major league scout; Mike Mondelli (No. 27) now a Nashville judge; and Roy Carter (No. 11) now a Nashville minister.

Schmittou congratulates one of his early sandlot stars, pitcher Wayne Garland, who would go on to major league fame. Garland has just pitched his team to second place in the Babe Ruth World Series.

Schmittou continued to play while he coached. Here he waits on the mound for a signal during a 1974 City League All-Star game. Coaching first is Roger Davis, who, with one leg, gained fame as a wheelchair basketball player.

Schmittou debates the call of umpire Hester Gibbs in a Babe Ruth All-Star game in Lebanon...and loses

Schmittou with some of the stars on his 1968 Connie Mack team, which came in third in the World Series. Front row, left to right: Jerry Reasonover, who was All-SEC at Vanderbilt; Hardy Lavender, All-Gulf Coast Conference; and future major league star Wayne Garland. Beside Schmittou is assistant coach Bill Ed Smith.

Schmittou and players Jeff Peeples (left) and Ray Moss brought home the 1969 Connie Mack World Series runner-up trophy.

Right: Schmittou with his 1968 Connie Mack assistant coaches, Bill Ed Smith and Bobby Reasonover.

Schmittou took time out from baseball long enough to win the hand of his high school sweetheart, Shirley Reynolds. They were wed November 29, 1959.

Above: Schmittou with his 1969 Vanderbilt baseball team, which started a string of 10 straight 20-win seasons. His 11-year Vanderbilt record of 308-220-4 still ranks 17th among all-time coaching records.

Left: Schmittou observes the national anthem prior to a Vanderbilt game in 1968. He now says he may have been praying for rain, considering the state of his first college team.

Above: Schmittou with his 1973 Vanderbilt team, which won the SEC championship and finished 8th in the nation.

Left: Schmittou earned SEC Baseball Coach of the Year in 1974, the same year Roy Skinner was named SEC Basketball Coach of the Year.

Right: Schmittou accepts congratulations from Vanderbilt athletic director Jess Neely (center) and Commodore Club director Bill Stewart.

Some of Vandy's biggest little fans: Ronnie, Debbie, and Mike Schmittou, the coach's kids.

Christmas at the Schmittou home was always a crowded time. Among these guests are *Tennessean* sports writer Jimmy Davy and photographer S.A. Tarkington.

After forming the Nashville Sounds, Schmittou didn't forget his Vandy roots. Here he presents a $10,000 check to Vanderbilt AD Roy Kramer (center), baseball coach Roy Mewbourne (left), and former assistant Roy Carter. Yankees owner George Steinbrenner paid Vandy to play the 1980 UT game at Greer Stadium.

Owens recalls Schmittou sighing and remarking, "Well, I guess that about finishes it."

But Burr Regen, owner of the J.B. Regen Construction Company, whose son Damon had been one of Schmittou's favorite players on the Vanderbilt football team, spoke up.

"That doesn't sound like the Larry Schmittou I know," said Regen. "We're going to lick this thing yet."

"Burr Regen saved us," says Schmittou.

"He's just one of many people who stepped forward when it looked like we had reached the end of our rope and helped us keep going."

Regen suggested that Schmittou try to find ways to cut costs and get the price down. He said they might start by trying to wrangle some discounts on building materials.

"The first person I contacted was Eph Hoover, who owned a big cement company," says Schmittou. "Again, my coaching contacts came into play. Eph's son, Tommy, had played for me when I was freshman coach at MBA.

"I went to see Eph, and when I walked into his office he was putting a golf ball into a paper cup. Without looking up, he said, 'What do you want, Larry?'

"I got straight to the point. I said I wanted him to give me several thousand yards of concrete to help me build a baseball stadium.

"Eph got straight to the point, too. He said, 'You gotta be crazy. I can't do that.'

"But next day he called me and said, 'Look, if you can get Herbert Materials to donate the sand and some of the other stuff, and Marquette to donate the actual concrete, I'll do it for you.'

"I knew some people at both places, made some calls, and sure enough, they agreed to do it. So did Arlies Green, who had a caulking company.

"They did it simply out of friendship and because they felt like a stadium would be good for the city. The only thing they asked of us was to keep them in mind when we got our team. And I did. I always try to repay loyalty."

Not a single contractor turned down Schmittou's request for free or discounted materials. When he was finished, he had managed to chip around $200,000 off the original projected cost.

Next, Schmittou brazenly decided to ask the city for a $200,000 loan.

"I went to see the mayor, Richard Fulton, and he said, 'I don't know if I can get involved in that,'" says Schmittou. "So Buster Boguskie, who had helped me with the Council earlier, agreed to sponsor the loan request. I personally contacted each Council member to explain why I needed the loan and how I planned to pay it back in 10 years, with interest.

"Amazingly, considering all the trouble I'd had with the Council earlier, the loan approval sailed through. I kept my promise and repaid the loan early."

The stadium drive received another major boost when the Herschel Greer family donated $50,000 to the effort.

"All the time we were selling advance tickets, so we had some revenue coming in," says Schmittou. "We didn't waste a cent. Our 'office' was a 4-by-6 shack we built for about $500. It had one door, no window, no bathroom, and one light. None of us were on salary.

"When it snowed, the snow came through the cracks in the walls. It was bitter cold that winter. Farrell Owens and I sometimes would have to use cigarette lighters to thaw the lock on the door when we'd come to work in the morning.

"I hired a part-time secretary, Mrs. Jeanne Carney, who is still with us, for $3 an hour, and she and Shirley would man the 'office' while I was handling my coaching duties at Vanderbilt and Farrell was coaching at Pearl-Cohn.

"Not only was the cold weather delaying construction, but we ran into bedrock, and that meant more delays and expensive blasting.

"I'll always remember the winter of '77 as a long, cold, miserable one. But gradually the stadium began to take shape.

"So we had a team, and we were going to have a stadium. And I realized that, despite all the headaches we'd been through, we were going to have baseball in Nashville.

"Larry Schmittou didn't bring baseball to Nashville; Larry Schmittou and his friends did."

Chapter V
Opening Night Jitters

*"Baseball is a game where you are first
taken to the ball park by your mother and father,
and in later years you take them."*

Finally it was springtime, April 26, 1978. Opening night at Greer Stadium for the Nashville Sounds. And Larry Schmittou was not sure if he was watching a dream come true or nightmare unfold.

"If something could go wrong, it did go wrong," says Schmittou. "It seemed like it had been that way all winter as we encountered one obstacle after another. Almost every day someone from codes department would show up with some kind of new complaint. We'd just toss 'em in a pile and keep going."

The day before the grand opening, which would culminate two years of working, hoping, planning, and sacrifice, Schmittou was hit with the devastating news of his mother's death. Jane Ann Schmittou, who some 30 years earlier had taken her son to his first baseball game at Sulphur Dell, died after a long illness.

"Her death was not unexpected," says Schmittou, "but

when it actually happened, it was still awfully tough. It hit me hard."

That emotional blow came on top of mounting personal pressure on Schmittou, who had spent the winter battling stadium cost overruns and other snags while at the same time trying to drum up support for the team and sell tickets.

"All the while, I was still coaching baseball at Vanderbilt," says Schmittou. "A lot of days—most, actually—I was putting in 20-hour days."

But somehow he had persevered and pulled off the massive building project. And he had landed a team—the Class AA Cincinnati Reds—and gained membership in the Southern League.

Now that Herschel Greer Stadium was complete—well, almost—the team was ready to take the field, and a crowd was forming at the gates, ready and anxious to see Nashville sports history in the making.

Baseball was poised to make its return.

Electricity was in the air.

Unfortunately, there was no electricity in the wires that led to the stadium.

"Five minutes before the gates were scheduled to open, we got the electricity turned on," says Schmittou. "Five minutes. That's cutting it pretty close.

"We were also rushing to get the water and sewer lines run, and that was close, too. We got the water turned on the day before we opened. We were able to get only a couple of restrooms ready, so we rented a bunch of Port-O-Lets, which we spread around.

"I remember when they turned on the electricity, one lady went to the restroom, came out, and said, 'It's a nice restroom, Larry, but don't touch the walls or you'll get shocked.'

"I had the electrician check it out and he found that a ground wire had been run wrong. We got it fixed before anybody got electrocuted going to the restroom."

Schmittou's ground crew consisted of some of his Vanderbilt friends, Bill Kelly and Richard Baker. But there almost wasn't any grass to tend.

"Their pay was what they could eat and drink," says Schmittou, adding with a chuckle, "I think we lost money on Kelly, considering all his trips to the concession stands."

"We had a terrible winter, with 30-some-odd consecutive days when it never got above freezing," says Schmittou. "That not only put construction behind, but because of the extreme cold most of the sod we had put down died. We finally located some more in Dyersburg and put in a rush order. It arrived the day before we were scheduled to open, and I didn't see any way we could possible get it laid in time.

"Farrell Owens had an idea. He called some of the local radio stations and asked them to spread the word that we were having a sod party that night. The public was invited to come out and help lay sod.

"Between 9 that night and 2 in the morning, we had probably 400 volunteers show up to work. One guy, Richard Taylor, must have sat on a roller we'd borrowed for 15 straight hours, rolling sod to get it down.

"Why did they do it? It was like everybody wanted to pitch in and show that this was their ball park and their team."

Opening night had already been delayed and pushed back as far as it could be pushed.

"We played our first 15 or 16 games on the road, including some that were scheduled at our place," says Schmittou. "I paid Chattanooga $800 a game to swap some dates so we could play there. We put it off as long as we could, and now it was time to open the gates—ready or not."

The scheduled home opener on April 25 had been rained out, moving the big night back one day.

"We needed that extra 24 hours," says Schmittou. "I was still hiring concession workers the morning of the game. If it hadn't rained us out the night before, there was no way we could have opened. That was one time I was glad to have a rainout."

As it was, an hour before the gates opened, a bulldozer was still frantically smoothing dirt around third base and the finishing touches were being applied to the backstop.

Although Schmittou had been selling advance tickets all winter, a large portion of the crowd of 7,000 that first night simply showed up and bought their ticket at the gate.

"My staff and I arrived with about $25 in change," says Schmittou. "We had no idea what to expect. And of course we had made no provision to handle all the money that was coming in. People were buying tickets, souvenirs, programs, concessions . . . and the money was piling up.

"Remember, we didn't even have an office completed at the time. So as we collected money we just stuffed it in bags. We didn't even count it. I thought the bank would do that. We stuffed the money into bags, took it home, and the next day took it to First Tennessee Bank and told them to deposit it.

"They said, 'Have you counted it?'

"And I said, 'No, I thought that's what the banks did.'

"The next night we did the same thing. The third night we had an even bigger crowd and more money—about $20,000— and we didn't have any place to lock it up. I didn't want to take that much money home with me."

At around 1 a.m., Schmittou called a friend, Roy McDonald, an official with Commerce Union Bank, who was also a well-known Nashville umpire.

"I explained that we had all this cash and didn't know what to do with it," says Schmittou. "Roy said he'd come over and see what he could do.

"The first thing we did was get some big popcorn cans and divide the money according to denomination: $1's, $5's, $10's, $20's. Then we sorted all the loose change. By then it was about 2:30 in the morning.

"We loaded up our popcorn cans of money and went to

one of McDonald's branch banks, located at the corner of Third and Broadway. Roy and I and a Metro policeman who was working as a security guard pulled up and began to carry in our cans of money.

"At the time there was a massage parlor located across the street and some of the girls were sitting out front watching us. A couple of winos stumbled out of an alley to see what was going on. I guess they wondered what somebody was doing at 2 in the morning carrying popcorn cans into a bank while a security guard kept watch.

"We finally got it all deposited, and on the way home about dawn I began to realize there was going to be more to running a baseball team than I'd figured."

The stadium had been named after Herschel Greer, a long-time Nashville business and civic leader. Greer was the first president of Vols Inc. when the professional baseball club was fan-owned between 1959 and 1963.

Greer, who died at age 69 on March 19, 1976, was one of the state's foremost real estate mortgage bankers and a founder of Guaranty Mortgage Company. His son, H. Lynn Greer Jr., and his wife, Mary Martha Greer, had made a $25,000 matching gift to the stadium fund-raising drive. The Guaranty Insurance Agency would match the gift.

"We felt Daddy would be right out there selling tickets if he were here," said the younger Greer in announcing the donation. "Baseball was his game. He liked many sports, but baseball was always his favorite."

A former coaching friend of Schmittou's, Ralph Brown, helped secure the Greer family's support.

In 1958 Greer helped organize Vols Inc., a corporation to keep professional baseball in Music City. Despite his efforts, the Nashville Vols folded in 1963. The historic Sulphur Dell ball park, constructed in 1885, christened by Grantland Rice in 1907, and host to such legends as Babe Ruth, was demolished in 1969.

Now Greer's family had helped bring pro baseball back to life in Nashville.

"That was obviously an important donation," says Schmittou. "But I felt it was fitting that the stadium be named in honor of Mr. Greer not just because of the gift but because of his love for baseball in Nashville. I don't know of anybody who had worked harder for it over the years than he had."

Schmittou decided to allow the fans to cast votes to decide the new team's nickname. A total of 287 different suggestions poured in, and "Sounds" was declared the winner.

At the time, the term "Nashville sound" was prominent in the international recording industry.

There was some sentiment toward naming the team the Vols in nostalgic tribute to the city's bygone baseball team, but many—especially Vanderbilt fans—felt that name smacked too strongly of the University of Tennessee.

"I was open to Stars or Notes or Hits or Strings, which were among the finalists," says Schmittou, "but not Vols. No ball team of mine was going to be named Vols."

Schmittou himself sketched the team logo: a caricature of an old-time baseball player taking a swing at a baseball with a guitar. (Today the Sounds logo is still one of the top 10 in minor-league baseball, based on sale of items it appears on.)

"What's the one thing Nashville is famous for worldwide? Country music," explains Schmittou. "I wanted to give our ball club as strong a Nashville flavor as possible.

"I made a rough drawing of what I had in mind, then took it to an artist for the finished product."

From the madness of Opening Night throughout the remainder of the season, the Greer Stadium turnstiles never stopped spinning. Nashville would lead all minor-league teams in attendance that season, drawing 380,159 fans for 57 dates, an average of 6,669 per game.

The Sounds weren't simply a success; they were a national

phenomenon, attracting attention from Sports Illustrated to the Sporting News and New York Times.

Schmittou had disproved the doubters and quieted the critics, who said baseball was dead forever in Nashville. Baseball was back, big-time.

The fans poured in and the awards piled up.

Schmittou was named the Sporting News Class AA and Southern League Executive of the Year in 1978 and again in 1980. Those same years he won the coveted Larry McPhail Award for the best overall minor-league operation.

More important, says Schmittou, was Greer Stadium's growing national reputation as a minor-league mecca.

After the fan explosion the first season, Schmittou quickly added more seats the following year—mortgaging his home for $100,000 to help pay for the additions—and still the stadium often overflowed.

The Sounds, in their second season, drew 515,676, an average of 8,108 per game.

Even Schmittou was awed.

"For the first time in my life I had underestimated my abilities," says Schmittou. "In all my years of coaching I had all the confidence in the world. But this was my first really business experience, where I was the boss on a day-to-day basis.

"I was dealing with bankers, lawyers, and politicians. With each day I gained more confidence and learned from my mistakes.

"With each home stand I learned more about what the fans wanted, what we were doing right, and what we were doing wrong.

"I used lessons from a man I'd observed and admired greatly, Ray Danner, the founder of Shoney's. My wife, who had run a day-care center while I was coaching, had kept Ray Danner's child, and I had become acquainted with him.

"He knew I was struggling financially back then, so he made me a 'Shoney's spy.' My wife and I would eat at a different Shoney's and we would rate the meal, the courtesy of the waitress, the cleanliness of the restaurant and restrooms, and overall service. That stuck in my mind, how to treat customers.

"I tried to follow his example. I always go out and meet the fans, shake hands, and talk with them. I ask them how we're doing, and I listen to what they have to say. Ray Danner taught me to listen to my customers, to let them know I care about them.

Schmittou's "customers" continued to flock to the stadium in record droves. Schmittou theorizes several factors contributed to the surging attendance.

"First of all, baseball was new to Nashville after a 15-year absence," he says. "The community was hungry for it.

"I think we did a good job coming up with a team name and logo that identified with the city.

"And we were fortunate to have signed with Cincinnati, which at that time was one of the hottest teams in the major leagues. We had done some surveys and found that the Reds had a lot of fans in our area.

"Our first manager, Chuck Goggin, was a very positive person who got involved in the community. The players were cooperative and worked well with the fans. They became a part of the community. Some of those first players still live in Nashville."

Then there were the wild and crazy promotions, which earned Schmittou a national reputation as the P.T. Barnum of baseball: Tight-Fittin' Jeans contests (in tribute to team co-owner Conway Twitty's hit song), Used-Car Night, in which some fans won a used car. Some were in good shape, some weren't. One night the winner looked at the clunker he had just won and refused to accept the keys to it.

On Vegas Night, the fan holding the winning ticket received an expense-paid trip for two to Vegas. The catch: they were whisked away immediately from the stadium to the airport and put on the plane.

On Ice Cream Night, Sounds fans were treated to a 360-foot-long banana split.

The musical Annie was a hit at the time, and Schmittou held an "Annie Look-a-Like contest." It drew 195 girls and one boy.

"I did the boy a favor and got him out of there," chuckles Schmittou.

Money Scramble Night offered a fan a chance to collect up to $10,000. That's how much was scattered over the Greer Stadium field in $1 bills. One bill was marked with an X and was worth $1,000. The fan had one minute to grab all he could grab.

Schmittou also created a mascot, "Homer Horsehide." It was a young woman who wore an outfit that consisted of a plastic head in the form of a giant baseball.

Homer Horsehide was doing well until Bat Night.

"Homer became a target for every little kid with a bat," says Schmittou. "They liked to have killed her."

"We tried to make Greer Stadium a fun place to go," says Schmittou. "In those early years, especially, it sort of became the 'in' place to be. It was good, clean fun for the whole family. People of all ages could come to the ball game, eat a hot dog, sing along with 'Elvira,' and compete for prizes.

"The baseball was almost a bonus."

Looking back, Schmittou says he over-promoted during that period.

"If I had it to do over, I wouldn't have used up all those promotions in those first years," says Schmittou. "I'd have saved some for later. You can't keep doing the same promotions over and over because they get stale, and I wished I had kept some so they'd be fresh.

"But I took the 'insurance policy' of adding the promotions, and they helped add to what I think would probably have been big crowds anyway."

Community pride was also part of the lure.

"Everybody had been hearing and reading for about two years how this wouldn't work," says Schmittou. "I think a lot of people came out to support me and the team.

"The little guy on the street, the one I've always associated myself with, said, 'To heck with the critics. I'm for the guy who's bucking the odds.'

"Those early years were exciting ones. I knew I had a winner."

Yet, years later when he looks back on that long-ago Opening Night and the frantic first season, Schmittou admits, "If I had known then what I know now, I doubt that I'd have the courage to go through with it. I had absolutely no idea what I was getting into."

Schmittou once told Nashville's Adva*ntage* magazine:

"If I had to do it over again, I wouldn't do it. Period. I have created a monster within my own self, and I find myself not doing some of the things I might go back and do—especially enjoying my family.

"This has tremendously changed my whole life. I went from a bubble-gum-chewing third base coach to a high-blood-pressure businessman who worries about things other than whether to bunt or hit-and-run."

On further reflection, however, Schmittou admits he really has no regrets, that the personal sacrifice has been worth it.

"Running a baseball club is not as much fun as coaching," he says, "but it sure as heck pays more."

The payment to which he refers is not just money.

"When I stand by that entrance at night, or walk through the stands, and some fan says, 'Thanks for everything you've done for baseball' . . . well, that makes it all worthwhile.

"Who knows? Some little kid may come to Greer Stadium with his dad or mom, the way I used to go to the Sulphur Dell with my mama. And someday he may look back and treasure that trip to my ball park the way I still look back and treasure those memories of going with my mama.

"That's what baseball is all about."

CHAPTER VI
MINOR DETAILS

"The only time nothing can happen in your life
is when you do nothing."

L arry Schmittou's fame as a minor-league genius execu
tive quickly spread.

One day he got a call from Bobby Bragan, at the time the
president of the whole minor-league organization. He was asking for Schmittou's help.

"He said, 'Larry, we've got a team in trouble in Class A
ball. Would you like to buy it?'

"The team was in Charleston, South Carolina. It owed
$7,000 in 'blue book' baseball debt, travel expenses, and so
on. I called a coaching friend of mine down there and asked
about the Charleston operation. He said the park was awful
and suggested that if we bought the team we should move it
somewhere else.

"I called Bob Teitlebaum, a sportswriter I knew in Roanoke,
Virginia, and asked what he thought would be a good location
for a minor-league team in the Carolinas. He said Greensboro,
North Carolina, would be ideal.

"So my investors and I bought the team and leased a park

in Greensboro. That was the start of us getting involved in acquiring teams."

In addition to Greensboro, Schmittou and his partners would go on to own teams in Eugene, Oregon; Daytona Beach, Florida; Salem, Virginia; Huntsville, Alabama; Salt Lake City, Utah; Wichita, Kansas; and Winston-Salem, North Carolina.

Along with his various teams, Schmittou collected some interesting stories.

"We had great success at Greensboro, which hadn't had baseball in 15 years, so it was easy to be successful," says Schmittou. "From there, word got out to Durham that I might be interested in putting a team there.

"I went to check out the park, and it was really old and run-down. It hadn't been used in 20 years. The seats were falling apart, there were no concession stands, and grass had taken over the warming track.

"Our group kept asking to see the clubhouse and the guy showing us around kept putting it off. It was clear he didn't want us to go in and look around. But finally, after we kept insisting, he agreed.

"He unlocked the door and we walked in. The biggest rat I've seen in my life went right over our feet. We decided right then our tour of the park was over.

"We went to see the mayor to see how much the city was willing to spend to fix up the place, and I told him about 14 things that needed doing. He wanted to know how much it would cost, and when I told him about a half-million dollars he said he'd get back to me. I never heard from him again."

Another party, Miles Wolff, who didn't share Schmittou's aversion to rats, later took control of the club. He made the Durham Bulls operational, and when the park became the setting of the Hollywood blockbuster, Bull Durham, it was suddenly the nation's most famous minor-league team.

Schmittou next turned his attention to Salem, Virginia.

"I went and visited and they had a nice little park," he recalls. "I looked it over, met with three of the owners, and they arranged for me to meet with the mayor in the back of Tarpley's Furniture Store. It's a restaurant in the back of an actual furniture store, and anybody who's anybody in Salem eats lunch at Tarpley's.

"We went in and they talked to me about buying the club, but I couldn't get a price out of them. Finally one of the gentlemen came over with a piece of scrap paper and handed it to me.

"He said, 'We've decided we like you and would like to sell you the team. We have a price for you.'

"I said, 'Really? What is it?'

"He said, '$16,688.17'

"I said, 'That's good. I'll take it. But how did you come up with that figure?'

"He said, 'That's what we owe the popcorn company.'

"That, and one other bill, was what they owed, and that's how they decided what to sell the team for."

"After buying his third baseball team, in 1982 Schmittou bought a hockey team for Nashville.

"Our mayor, Richard Fulton, was on me to do it to help out Municipal Auditorium," says Schmittou. "I went in blind on it, but that led to the purchase of baseball teams number four and number five.

"We were at an All-Star hockey game in Salt Lake City that winter, and snow was everywhere. One morning, with nothing else to do, I decided to go for a walk. I asked the desk clerk where the baseball park was, and he said down the street a few blocks.

"I walked down to have a look, and I was immediately impressed by the place. It was a beautiful setting, with the mountains all around. As I wandered around, a young woman walked up and I introduced myself.

"She said, 'I know who you are. You're the owner of Nashville, Greensboro, and Salem.' Turned out, she was the team's general manager.

"We talked awhile and she said, 'Why don't you buy this club?'

"I said, 'Who's the owner?' She told me it was Joe Gagliardi, and I said, 'Well, go get him on the phone.'

"She called him up and I said, 'I understand you've got a team for sale.'

"He just said, 'Yeah.'

"I said, 'Well, what do you want for it?'

"He said, '$430,000 and I ain't taking one penny less.'

"I said, 'I'll buy it. Give me two or three days to get the money together.'

"By the time I walked back to my hotel, I had a call waiting. It was the owner. He said, 'The club's yours. We're going to close next week.'

"Understand, I had less than two months before opening day. I decided to do the best I could, so I visited the Mormon Church and saw how family-oriented Salt Lake City is. I made plans to designate every Monday as Family Night, and it would turn out to be a great success."

The next day Schmittou received a call from Bob Freitas. He had formed a company that bought and sold minor-league franchises.

"He said, 'I've got a franchise in Eugene, Oregon, that you need to buy. It's a short-season Class A team that doesn't start play until June.'

"He said they wanted $75,000 for the team, and he said it was a gold mine. So I caught a plane, flew to Oregon, and looked it over.

"It was an old wood ball park and when I walked in I heard this strange 'Hoot, hoot, hoot!'

"I found out that pigeons were a big problem in the park, so they put these fake hoot owls in the stadium to scare them off.

"I figured at $75,000 I couldn't go wrong. Next day, we closed on both Salt Lake City and Eugene, Oregon. I got two ball clubs because I decided to take a walk in the snow to look at a ball park."

Schmittou quickly realized he was having to spend too much time on the road, supervising his two far-flung teams.

"I recognized really quick that Salt Lake City and Eugene were just too far away from my base in Nashville, so I told my general managers if I got the right offer I'd sell.

"In two months we sold Salt Lake for a half-million-dollars profit—after we'd made $200,000 for the club. Then I sold Eugene for $150,000—twice what I'd paid for it, and after that club had also made money.

"Bob Beban was my general manger in Eugene and he did a great job. He is still there. I sold Eugene to Dave Elmore, who owns six minor-league teams and two hockey teams. I'm still proud to call him my friend.

"A month later I got an offer from two guys in New York for $150,000 for Salem. In three months we went from owning five teams to two."

In 1984 when Nashville went Class AAA, Schmittou had to figure out what to do with his Class AA franchise.

"The Southern League wanted me to just give it to them, but at that time Class AA franchises were going for $300,000 to $400,000 and I said, 'To heck with that.' I decided, with the help of Southern League president and friend Jimmy Bragan, to move the Class AA franchise to another city.

"We had bought the Evansville franchise and I wanted to keep the lease on the stadium, so I planned to move my Class AA Nashville franchise there. But the Southern League didn't want me to, so I went down and visited with Huntsville, Alabama."

Huntsville wanted the team but didn't want to permit beer sales. Schmittou said no deal.

"Shortly after that they called and agreed to sell beer everywhere except in one designated nondrinking section. We wound up selling two season tickets in the nondrinking section."

Schmittou continued to search for a team for Evansville. He landed a franchise for $15,000 but nine months later received a call from an owner wanting to buy the team. He paid Schmittou $100,000 for it.

"We made $85,000 on the Evansville club and never had an employee or played a game," says Schmittou.

Schmittou got a team in the Florida State League to help out the Rangers, but his experience with Daytona Beach was not a good one.

"I knew from studying the demographics that it wasn't a good area," he says. "There is a big letdown after major-league spring training, plus the average age of fans was a drawback. One night we had Jacket Night, and only two kids showed up.

The Rangers, as planned, eventually took the team off Schmittou's hands.

He then set his sights on the Texas League.

"I got an offer for a team in Beaumont and we paid $500,000 for it, with the understanding I could move it to New Orleans. Then I got a lesson in New Orleans politics.

"I was trying to arrange to play some games in the Superdome for $3,000 a game, and I thought we had a deal done. But I kept waiting for final approval and after I didn't hear anything for several days I knew something was wrong.

"I called down there and was told a certain judge whose vote was needed to approve the deal had made it known he would like a piece of the team—for free. That was the end of my dealings with New Orleans."

Schmittou next landed at Wichita, Kansas.

"They had a nice little park but they also had the National Baseball Congress, an amateur league from several states that was really popular there.

"When I inspected the park I found it had a pigeon problem, kinda like Eugene, Oregon. In fact, that was why it was for sale. The owner's wife came to the park one night straight from the beauty shop, and a pigeon flew over and ruined her new hairdo. That was the last straw. Her husband decided to sell."

Schmittou bought the team, only to learn that the pigeons weren't his only problem.

"The National Baseball Congress was so popular that it was creating scheduling conflicts with the minor-league team," he says. "Finally I had a chat with the NBC president and said, 'This thing isn't going to work. One of us needs to own both operations.'

"He said, 'Name me a price.'

"I told him $1.2 million, and he referred me to Bob Rich, who took it. Rich owns the Buffalo Bisons, along with some businesses in Middle Tennessee, and has done a tremendous job with all his operations. Like Dave Elmore, I consider Bob a close friend."

Schmittou, who owned Greensboro, also wanted a team in Columbus, but the Southern League blocked it because he would have owned two teams in the same league.

"I got mad and one day I got a call asking if I'd sell Greensboro and my option on Columbus," says Schmittou. "I'd paid $14,000 for Greensboro; he offered me $1.2 million. I took it."

Schmittou also dabbled with a team in Winston-Salem. He made a $25,000 down payment on a $125,000 asking price, but at the last minute the owner backed out. Several years later he made an offer again, and this time the sale went through. Shortly afterward Schmittou sold the team for a $1 million profit.

About that time he also set in motion plans to sell Huntsville for $5 million.

"I just decided I needed to pull in my boundaries and concentrate more on Nashville and our major-league push," says Schmittou.

But not before he would make one more minor-league purchase in a most unique arrangement: He would put both a Class AA and Class AAA team in Greer Stadium at the same time.

"It happened because of major-league expansion," says Schmittou. "The two clubs that were chosen to go as Class AAA affiliates were Charlotte and Ottawa. That meant that in 1993 Charlotte had a Class AA team floating around.

"Southern League president Jimmy Bragen called and asked about putting the team in Winston-Salem, but I said that wouldn't work because of the facility. I said I might consider putting it in Nashville.

"I asked my son Ronnie and PR director Jim Ballweg what they thought about it, and they were all for it. So we agreed to do it."

Nashville's Class AAA parent club, the Chicago White Sox, didn't like the idea, but Schmittou finally convinced the Sox that two Greer Stadium schedules could be worked out without conflict.

The name Nashville Xpress was settled on because of the railroad tracks that run near the park and because the team was roaring into town like a freight train. And the Xpress was ready to play in 1993.

"There was some concern that the Xpress would take away from the Sounds attendance," says Schmittou. "But fortunately we had two good teams that season and attendance didn't suffer. We drew 630,000, which was 120,000 more than we'd drawn the year before with just one team.

"Our season ticket holders were given the option of buying an Xpress ticket for $100 on top of their Sounds ticket. Other tickets were sold on game day."

Schmittou said some local media criticized the two-team deal, "because they didn't want to cover it. And they claimed it watered down the product. But we had fun doing it."

At the end of the season, Dennis Basteen reached an agreement to buy the Xpress, provided he could move it to Lexington, Kentucky. He ran into what Schmittou terms "political resistance," however, and couldn't get his ball park built. He asked Schmittou to keep the team in Nashville one more year.

"The worst fear I had was what if both teams are bad?" says Schmittou. "We'd been lucky the first year because both teams were good, plus there was the newness and all."

Once again, fate or fortune smiled on Schmittou. One of the Xpress' opponents in 1994 was the Birmingham Barons, who had signed Michael Jordan, and the team was basking in the national spotlight. When the Barons and Jordan came to Greer Stadium, the spotlight—and crowds—followed.

"Jordan played 10 games in Nashville and consequently the team was a financial success," says Schmittou. "His first three games here he drew so many fans that we probably paid expenses for the Xpress' entire year. The down side was that he took away from the Sounds' attention."

Still, total attendance was up, and Schmittou says that was his bottom line.

After that second season, however, Schmittou decided two years of two teams was enough, "because the media kept taking potshots at me, and I just didn't want to take the chance with two teams again."

The Xpress left Nashville and eventually landed in Port City, South Carolina, where it changed its name to the Roosters.

Nashville and Schmittou were back down to just one team.

In addition to professional baseball, Schmittou also tried his hand at hockey and basketball.

"In 1981 our group revived minor-league hockey in Nashville," he says. "The old Dixie Flyers had been gone for several years, and at the urging of the mayor and some of the other owners, we got a team in the Central Hockey League.

"We were an affiliate of the Minnesota North Stars. After a squabble with the Metro Council we got a lease where we also ran the concessions, but minor-league hockey was not very strong at the time, and the whole league folded.

"The next year we got into what is now the East Coast Hockey League, which had only five teams and was really shaky. At the end of the season we sold the team to another party and got out of the hockey business."

In 1990, at the behest of an old Vanderbilt coaching friend, Ron Bargatze, Schmittou entered the world of professional basketball. Nashville landed a franchise in the new Global League, with Schmittou's support.

"Even though our local 'expert sportswriter' Larry Woody had insisted we should get a Continental Basketball Association team, the Municipal Auditorium commission awarded the contract to the Global League," says Schmittou. "The team was supposed to play Russia and a lot of other foreign teams. Boy, I wish we had listened to Woody. We lost about $300,000 or $400,000 on our team. The 'Bad News Bears' team of baseball was mild compared with that basketball team.

"We once actually picked up a player on the corner of the street in Greensboro, North Carolina, and added him to the roster. Another time, we had a game rained out. The roof at the Auditorium had sprung a leak and water was all over the floor.

"We drew so few people that we finally moved to Jackson, Tennessee, and did pretty well there. We got our roster down to just eight players, and they won the league championship. I wish they hadn't, because that meant we had to spend more money on championship rings for the players."

The next year the Global League mercifully expired, saving Schmittou and his partners further financial agony.

CHAPTER VII
OFF TO TEXAS

"Never show your true emotions,
because it might scare you to death."

In 1983 the major leagues came calling. Schmittou was hired by the Texas Rangers of the American League to serve as vice president of marketing and administration.

He packed his bags and headed for Texas.

"It came totally unexpected," says Schmittou.

"Over the past five years our Nashville franchise had been very successful and got a lot of national attention. By this time we had owned five different baseball teams and a hockey team, and with each of those we had been able to put fannies in the seats. That was the name of the game.

"I'd earned a reputation for promotions and marketing, and I'd also made a lot of friends and connections with officials and scouts on various teams. I'd had some overtures but nothing that really appealed to me.

"One morning—it was February 12, 1983—I came to my office and had a message to call Joe Klein of the Texas Rangers. Klein had been named general manager of the Rangers about 60 days earlier. I knew Joe vaguely. I had spent maybe three or four minutes talking to him in my entire life.

"I called Joe back and he said, 'I'll bet you've never been propositioned this early in the morning.'

"Joe, who had just hired Doug Rader as manager, said, 'Larry, we need someone to turn this club around in attendance and get us out of debt. It is a tough job. Would you do me the favor of coming down and discussing it with our owner, Eddie Chiles, tomorrow?'

"Keep in mind, this is less than two months before the season started. I said, 'As a favor to you, Joe, I will, but I don't know that I'd have an interest this close to the season.' "

Still, in the back of his mind, Schmittou considered the Rangers' position, "an opportunity that fit my mold. They had no history of success. Like when I came to Vanderbilt, they had no way to go but up. When I started the Sounds, they had no way to go but up. When I bought Greensboro, they had no way to go but up. When I bought the hockey team, it had no way to go but up. The Rangers met that same criteria.

"So I made a plane reservation and didn't tell anyone but my wife that I was going.

"George Dyce, who had come to work for the Sounds after the '78 season after being an unpaid volunteer, was over visiting one of our other clubs in Salem, Virginia. I called him and told him I was going to be out of town the next day.

"I flew to Texas and arrived at the Rangers office, where I met the owner, Mr. Chiles, for the first time. I didn't know anything about him except that he'd made a fortune in oil and had run some political ads.

"Joe said, 'Tell Mr. Chiles about the promotions and things you've done.' I explained what we'd been doing at Nashville and some of our other clubs.

"Mr. Chiles told me a little about the Rangers' struggles and said he needed somebody in charge of marketing who could draw fans and start making money. Then out of the blue he said, 'How much money do you make?'

"I told him, and he and Joe talked a few minutes, then he offered me about $20,000 more than I was making. At that time, $20,000 represented a pretty good sum. I accepted the job.

"I called back home and told Shirley I'd taken the job. The Sounds were in good shape—all our clubs were in good shape—and I knew George Dyce, who I made general manager, was capable of looking after things.

"Working in the major leagues was something I'd always wanted to do. If I was going to make a career move, this was the time."

By the next day, word had already leaked in the media.

"I got a call from a Dallas sportswriter as soon as I got back to the office, asking me what I thought about becoming vice president of the Texas Rangers. I knew the cat was out of the bag.

"I immediately began calling my owners to set up a meeting to give them the news first-hand.

"I hadn't even told my kids, so I rushed home to catch them when they got home from school. Two jumped for joy and one, Susan, cried, because she didn't want to move away from her friends.

"Then I went back to my office to tell my employees. I could see the jubilation on the face of (head groundskeeper) Jim Anglea's face. He knew that was his ticket to the big leagues, because he was planning to go with me."

Later, when Schmittou had called his fellow owners together and broke the news of his impending departure, the reaction was mixed.

"Most of them were happy for me, but a couple were mad. It caught them by surprise," says Schmittou. "They were concerned about my leaving's effect on the Sounds' day-to-day operation, even though by then they had gotten back more than 100 percent of the money they had invested.

"This was something I wanted to do for Larry Schmittou,

and I wasn't going to let the partners dictate the rest of my life.

"I assured them I would still be in charge and would return to Nashville every time the Rangers were on the road. The fact that George Dyce would run the club in my absence made things smoother, because they all had confidence in him.

"I called Conway Twitty, who was on tour, and he congratulated me. He knew this was something I really wanted, and he couldn't have been nicer about it. He said if I ever needed anything while I was in Texas, all I had to do was give him a call."

When Schmittou left, he took popular Sounds announcer Chuck Morgan with him. Morgan was a Nashville DJ who also worked on the Grand Ole Opry, and his enthusiastic PA flair had been an immediate hit with Sounds' fans. Schmittou wanted Morgan to impart that same energy and excitement over the Rangers' PA system.

"I knew Chuck could put some life in the ball park," says Schmittou. "I called him, and he was enthusiastic about the move. He was among my first hires, and he's still there."

Schmittou also hired Dave Fendrick, whom he had met through baseball connections. To handle Rangers' promotions, he took Jackie Sullivan from the Sounds' advertising staff.

"Jackie asked to go," says Schmittou. "She saw it as a career opportunity."

When Schmittou arrived at his new office in Texas he learned that only about 1,400 season tickets had been sold for the upcoming season in 44,000-seat Arlington Stadium. And there were less than 60 days before opening day.

"The Rangers were coming off a last-place finish and the franchise had lost $8 million the previous year," says Schmittou. "As I said, I didn't have a hard act to follow. But I also knew I had a long way to go.

"Joe Klein helped me tremendously. He gave me some idea of what had been done right and what had been done wrong. I inherited the promotions, the media relations, the ticket sales, radio and TV, marketing, and several other departments.

"One thing that gave me hope was the fact that Mr. Chiles wanted to buy the ball park from the city. That would give us the freedom to do things the way we wanted to. I could control my own destiny.

"There was one guy who was working for the Rangers in a secondary role, who had done a lot of favors for me. His name was Bobby Bragan. They had kinda put Bobby out to pasture, but I knew he was a great speaker and he was well-known in the Dallas–Fort Worth area. He hads been the very successful manager of the Fort Worth Cats in the old Texas League before he became a major-league manager.

"I kinda latched onto Bobby, since public relations was one of my departments, and told him to get me into some places to speak. Before long he had me at every meat-and-three place in Fort Worth, and we started winning people back."

An old college baseball connection helped Schmittou sell tickets. Pitcher Rick Honeycutt, who Schmittou had wanted to sign at Vanderbilt but couldn't because the school wouldn't give him a scholarship, was pitching for the Rangers. The ex-UT star would have a tremendous year. He led the American league in earned run average that season.

"We jumped out of the gates fast," says Schmittou, "and by the All-Star break we were in first place by two games."

The improved play of the team, combined with Schmittou's marketing and promotions, kept the turnstiles spinning.

"We also eliminated some spending by cutting out a lot of things that were not baseball," says Schmittou. "We sold a cable TV deal and quit making Ranger Aid, which was supposed to put Gator Aid out of business but had become a joke. We got back to strictly baseball.

"We drew about 350,000 more paid attendance my first season than they had drawn the previous year, and we cut out a lot of expenses. We pretty much had a break-even year, financially, but that wasn't bad, considering they'd lost $8 million the year before."

At the end of the season, Chiles called Schmittou, Klein, and Charlie Wangner, the club's director of finance, to his office.

"He said, 'You all have done a tremendous job,' " recalls Schmittou.

"He gave us each an envelope and told us not to open it until later. Of course we all opened our envelopes five seconds after Mr. Chiles left. I discovered he had given me a $50,000 a year raise. He had done the same for Joe and Charlie.

"Mr. Chiles also gave Doug Rader, the manager, a raise, and gave us all gift certificates for new jackets worth about $1,000 each at a fancy clothing store.

"Rader was out of town at the time, so Joe and Charlie and I went down to get our jackets. Mine was a Western cut, which I didn't like, but Rader's wasn't, so I took his. I guess he liked mine, because he never said anything.

"The next day Mr. Chiles called us all back into his office and said, "You know, I've been thinking about yesterday. I hope you haven't opened those envelopes yet.'

"I thought, 'Uh-oh.'

"Mr. Chiles said, 'I've changed my mind. Here's another envelope.'

"I opened mine up and there was another $25,000 raise on top of the $50,000 one he had given us the day before. As we left, I joked to Joe, 'You know, if we keep getting raises like this every day, before long we'll be making pretty good money around here.' "

Despite the huge turnaround in attendance and Schmittou's $75,000-a-year raise, not everything was rosy in Texas.

Schmittou was having problems with some of the probing media, and a feud began that would continue to fester.

"The only negative thing I had seen—and I knew this going in—was that the Texas press was almost as negative as the Nashville press," says Schmittou.

"We faced a major obstacle in competing with the Dallas Cowboys for coverage. I was determined to change that.

"Part of the problem was that the print media wanted to run the press box, like they'd always done, and I wasn't going to let them. The radio and TV guys couldn't even come into the press box, and they understandably resented it. That hurt our coverage with them.

"There was a TV guy named Dale Hansen, who was always giving the Rangers heck. I called him up and said, 'Dale, I'm new here. Why are you so mad at the Rangers? Have we done something wrong?'

"He said, 'You don't let me in your press box. You treat me like a second-class citizen.'

"I told him I'd take care of it. I called Bobby Brown, who was president of the American League, and said, 'What's the deal here?' He said that going way back, when there was no radio and TV coverage, the sports writers ruled the press box.

"He said, 'If you want to change that, I'll back you.'

"That's how it all got started. I tried to treat all members of the media equally, and some sportswriters didn't like it."

Schmittou's biggest critics were Randy Galloway of the Dallas Morning News and Jim Reeves of the Fort Worth Star, president of the local chapter of the Baseball Writers Association.

Galloway christened Schmittou "Larry the Lizard," and "Larry (Not Your Lucky Number) Schmittou."

Galloway claimed Schmittou was a minor-leaguer "who came in here with some rinky-dink promotions you'd see in Gastonia."

The media criticized Schmittou for long concession-stand lines on opening night of 1984, after extensive stadium renovations.

"We were lucky to have any concession stands open at all," says Schmittou. "We had worked 72 straight hours—literally right up to game time—to get ready for the opener.

"We had just completed a 15-month project in five months.

"We had hired 1,200 new employees and went from 29 concession stands to 62. Nine of them weren't fully operational that first night and that's where most of the problems arose. Everything considered, I thought we did a pretty darned good job.

"I never paid any attention to Galloway and the other critics. I was running the show, not Galloway."

Schmittou found himself in the middle of another fuss over food.

"We didn't want to increase ticket prices, so the only other way to generate more revenue was through concessions," explains Schmittou. "In order to increase concession sales, we decided not to allow any outside food or beverage to be brought into the park. That upset some folks who had been used to bringing in their own food and drinks. It ruffled a few feathers at first, but they got used to it."

Galloway used the food squabble to take more shots at Schmittou, who eventually rescinded the rule against bringing in food—and the next year raised ticket prices to make up the lost revenue.

Amid all the criticism, Schmittou continued to make improvements.

After his first season, Schmittou decided Arlington Stadium needed a facelift to the tune of $6 million, plus another $4 million for a new Diamond-Vision TV scoreboard.

"I came up with a plan to pay for it," he says. "I was going to put up big boards in the outfield and sell advertisements like they had never been sold before. They would start at $60,000 and go on up.

"I also figured we could get two big ads for the scoreboard. I contacted Budweiser and two days later I was invited to St. Louis for a meeting. When I left, I had sold Budweiser one side of the scoreboard for $2.6 million, paid up front, in full. I then sold the other side to Marlboro for another $2.6 million. And we were on our way.

"We began to plan 52 more stadium suites, with the eight-seat suites going for $300,000 and the 12-seat suites going for $400,000. Within six months we had sold half of them and had more than enough money to start remodeling the stadium."

Things seemed to be going smoothly until Schmittou began to develop "philosophical differences" with Mike Stone, who had come aboard as the Rangers president and chief executive officer.

"Several things happened," says Schmittou.

"From the standpoint of how I was doing with the Rangers, things couldn't have been better. For example, Mr. Chiles called me in one day and said he was going to turn the concessions over to a company that was going to pay him $2 million for them plus 25 percent of the revenue; I asked him to give me 24 hours, then went out and sold the concessions for $6 million plus 40 percent. He wanted the money to buy out some limited partners.

"But still, I could see changes coming. Mr. Chiles was getting up in years and was giving up more and more control of the team. Mike Stone had come in as president and they had fired Joe Klein and named Tom Grieve new GM. Doug Rader and also been fired as the manager and was replaced by Bobby Valentine, who was a media darling.

"Gaylord bought one-third interest in 1984 and wanted the rest of it. Mike was concerned about how his role with the club would be changed if Gaylord took over, so he asked me to call George Gillette (a prominent businessman in Nashville who had expressed interest in sports franchises in the past) and ask him if he would be interested in the Rangers. I didn't do it; I felt that really wasn't my job. That was the first disagreement I had with Mike.

"Later, I had bought a team in Daytona Beach, Florida, with the understanding that the Rangers would eventually buy it from me and use it for their spring training site, after the Rangers bought the team and moved it to Port Charlotte. Stone,

without consulting me, sent some personnel down to Port Charlotte to run things and paid them more than some people who
were more experienced and who had been in the organization
longer. I told Mike I didn't think that was right. He didn't take it
very well. Mike and I began to have lunch together less and less
often, and things were never the same after that."

Even before the rift with the Rangers' new management,
Schmittou had made up his mind to return to Nashville.

"After the 1985 season, they wanted to sign me to a three-
year contract, but I wanted just one year at a time," says
Schmittou. "So at the end of the '86 season I had decided to
work one more year in Texas, then come home. We put our
house up for sale in July.

"At the end of November 1986, Stone called me into his
office and said I no longer fit in his plans. He thanked me for
what I had done for the Rangers. I told him that was fine, but
they had to pay me for the work I'd done to that point. They
ended up paying me for the '87 season, which I didn't work."

Stone announced to the public that Schmittou had been ter-
minated. Stone's statement read:

"The Texas Rangers announce today that Larry Schmittou,
the club's vice president for marketing and administration, will
not be offered a position with the organization for 1987. The
Rangers appreciate the tremendous efforts and accomplishments
that Larry Schmittou has made to turn Arlington Stadium into a
first-class facility. However, the demands and challenges that
face this franchise now and in the future require us to go into
another direction at this time."

"They're running me out of Texas," Schmittou told Bud
Burns, a writer with the *Tennessean* in Nashville. "I'm coming
home."

Ironically, Schmittou's dismissal came on the heels of a season
in which the Rangers finished a stunning second in the American League West Division and set a club attendance record, in-

creasing its turnout by almost 300,000 over 1985.

Even Schmittou's old nemesis, Randy Galloway, had to give him credit: "Larry brought in with him, or hired, some of the brightest people in the organization. These people are a big reason the organization is so successful.

"Schmittou is respected in many minor-league circles, especially by young people who want to get started in the business. They come to him as a learning process."

Chuck Morgan, who remained behind with the Rangers when Schmittou left, pointed out:

"A lot of the things we kept doing were things Larry brought with him and started. The attendance has been up because what he did worked."

"I was glad I went," says Schmittou, "but I was glad to be back home."

CHAPTER VIII
BIG-LEAGUE DREAMS

"You can't get a hit if you don't swing."

The main reason Schmittou had made up his mind to return home to Nashville—even before "philosophical differences" began to grow between him and the new Rangers' management—was because he was needed by his ball club.

"Before I left for Texas, I had set in motion our move toward Class AAA, which was part of my plan to put Nashville in contention for a future major-league team," says Schmittou.

"But some things just weren't running as smoothly as I'd hoped. I'd heard rumblings from some of my people at Greer Stadium that things really weren't the same, and that I needed to get back home.

"I was concerned about the Nashville franchise at that point. I was anxious to get back and make some stadium improvements and get our attendance back up.

"After the '85 season, prices jumped but attendance didn't. In '86 we didn't have a good team. I was not here to observe a change in managers and have a day-to-day conversation with the farm director. Also, I think—and this was nobody's fault— that Farrell Owens and I had created an image with the Sounds that wasn't there any more.

"We were always at the park, glad-handing, meeting the fans. That wasn't the personality of some of the people I had left in charge.

"I don't want to be unfair to George Dyce, when he was put into that position. It was like my situation years before when I had to follow Mr. Rutherford at Bailey Junior High. The personalities were different. George had to be his own person. He wasn't me. Had he tried to be me, that would be wrong. He had to be himself. And people were saying, 'We don't see him out in the stands like Schmittou was. The atmosphere is not the same.' Again, I certainly don't blame George for that. We were just different personalities.

"The bottom line was, attendance was down.

"Plus, I needed to do park improvements. I needed to do the final phase of Greer Stadium, which meant I had to go back before the Metro Council, meet with the bankers, and so on. If I was going to go $5 million in debt, I needed to be back on a day-to-day basis.

"While I was in Texas we had bought out five of the partners and that made us more of a smaller, on-the-same-page ownership group.

"We had done three expansions already at that point and still didn't have enough restrooms or parking, and we hadn't completed our suites. We had about $6.5 million invested in the park, and we owed no money. Now it was time to go back into debt.

"I also changed affiliation back to the Reds (from Detroit, which Nashville had joined after becoming a Class AAA club in 1985). And I started an architect drawing plans for a completed stadium. We wanted an enlarged seating area, better quality seats, more parking, a new press box. I thought it was all going to cost me about $3 million.

"We got the leading architect in the country on baseball stadiums and explained what all I wanted. I went to the bank and they agreed to loan me $2.5 million.

"We started demolishing in the fall of '87. By January the architect came in and said, 'I've got a small problem: You're going to have four beautiful new restrooms, but no water.'

"He explained that when we built the stadium we had put in a two-inch water line. We needed a four-inch line, and a pump. All of a sudden here's a half-million-dollar increase.

"Shortly after that the electrical contractor comes in and says the same thing: 'We need a bigger transformer' and all that stuff. Basically, we not only were making expansions, we were having to go back and correct some things we had done earlier. Before long, my $3 million project had become a $5 million project.

"I had exceeded the amount of money I could borrow from the local banks. They've gone as far as they can go, and they're getting upset at me coming back and asking for more. They won't go any further.

"Through some contacts, I approached Citicorp Bank, and a pretty good angel appears. It's one of the largest banks in the country. They approved our loan.

"So now I've got the financing to make the improvements, but in order to get it, my bank payments with interest, are over $100,000 a month.

"No one who has never laid their head on that pillow knowing that the meter is running on the interest and while they are sleeping they've run up about $2,000 more in debt can ever appreciate that feeling. Take my word for it: You don't sleep well.

"I once told somebody I slept like a baby through that stretch: I'd wake up crying about every half-hour."

Things got worse.

"We had a couple of big exhibition games with the Reds, and they got rained out. And our Sounds team that season was terrible. Attendance was down. So I've got a big debt and small crowds, which is not a good combination.

"But somehow we survive. By borrowing from Peter to pay Paul, we keep going. We get into '89 and again we don't have a very good team. We have five different managers, including one who managed only one game. The Reds are struggling, we're struggling, but we continue to keep going. I called in a lot of favors and a lot of friends helped out.

"Also, the owners were patient. Basically, from '84 on, they knew they weren't going to make a big profit up front. They were willing in invest in the future. We didn't take any money out of the ball club."

In fact, more money leaked out when Schmittou decided to buy back his concession contract. "We borrowed another $950,000 to buy back the concessions we had sold to Sportservice in 1985.

"We did it because our fans had told us they liked it better when we ran it. Our employees said they liked it better when we ran it. Bottom line: we thought we could do a better job.

"So after paying off about $1 million of our debt, we were now back almost $5 million in debt. I did it for our fans."

Finally, in 1990, Schmittou began to get some breaks.

"It was the most exciting season we ever had," says Schmittou. "We won a playoff game in 18 innings, after the entire season had been exciting. The crowds were back.

"Also, we applied for an expansion team and that had generated a lot of interest and enthusiasm. The media coverage was better, with the winning and the expansion push."

Schmittou admits that, in his heart of hearts, he really didn't expect Nashville to be awarded one of the two National League expansion teams.

"What I thought was that we could begin the process, get our name out, and get everything lined up and in order so that we would be in serious contention the next time expansion came up," he says.

"But as we went on, I thought we might have a better chance than I originally figured. I'd assumed Denver would be a shoo-in for one of the expansion teams, yet they were having ownership problems and ownership was one of the biggest criteria the Expansion Committee had set forth. So I figured that helped Nashville's chances."

The first thing Schmittou did was assemble a local ownership group capable of meeting the majors' $100 million net-worth requirement.

"Actually, we exceeded that," he says. "In terms of local ownership, we were in excellent shape."

The big hurdle was lack of a major-league stadium. Greer Stadium, with its cramped location, had no way to expand, especially in the critical area of parking. So Schmittou began to search for a site on which to build a new $40 million stadium. He found what he considered the perfect location, at the intersection of I-24 North and Briley Parkway.

He received assurances from the Bell Construction Company that a 42,000-seat stadium could be completed in less than 24 months.

What he needed next was a commitment from area fans that they would support a major-league team if he got one.

"We did all sorts of surveys and marketing studies," says Schmittou. "We found that the population base in our region was plenty large enough to support a team.

"There are 4.2 million people within a 120-mile radius of Nashville, and 1.6 million within a 60-mile radius. That's more than enough to support major-league baseball.

"So the demographics were excellent; our size is very comparable to the Kansas City, Milwaukee, and Cincinnati franchises, plus we have a wide-open TV market."

Schmittou felt there was one sure way to find out if fans would support a team: Ask them to make a commitment to buy a season ticket.

"If we proved we could sell tickets that would be a big plus for us in our presentation to the major leagues," he explains. "If we couldn't, well, we didn't deserve one."

Schmittou formed what he called his Dream Team—1,000 volunteers who agreed to fan out and collect ticket pledges. A season ticket to an 81-game home schedule would cost $700. Schmittou asked fans to put up a $100 deposit. The day Nashville was awarded a franchise, the other $600 would be due.

Why not simply ask for a $700 pledge, to be paid in full when a team was secured, rather than collecting $100 before the team passed go?

"I wanted to be certain we had firm commitments," says Schmittou. "If a fan were willing to make a $100 deposit, I would know he or she was serious. And their money was perfectly safe. If we didn't get a team, they would get it back." And they did.

The response was overwhelming. Schmittou had set a goal of 10,000 commitments. His Dream Team quickly exceeded that goal.

Meanwhile, he received the endorsement and support of then-governor Ned McWherter and other high-ranking Tennessee politicians such as Senators Jim Sasser and Al Gore Jr.

When the major-league owners held their annual meeting in Cleveland, Ohio, on June 14 and announced they were accepting expansion applications, Schmittou had his ready.

"I put it in the mail the first day and it was on (National League president) Bill White's desk the next morning," he says. "I wanted ours to be the first one in."

Schmittou's letter read:

Dear Bill:

I would like to request an expansion application for the city of Nashville for one of two expansion franchises in the National League.

As I mentioned in my previous letter, we feel that Nashville has done the best job in meeting the expansion criteria set forth in 1985, and we look forward to presenting our city for the National League's consideration.

Kindly mail the application to the Nashville Sounds Baseball Club, P.O. Box 23290, Nashville, Tennessee, 37202.
Sincerely,
Larry Schmittou
President, Nashville Sounds Baseball Club.

Schmittou then began to assemble a 120-page proposal, including color graphics and charts and illustrations detailing the area, ownership, marketing, and other information. He also put together a 30-minute video, narrated by Eddie Arnold, extolling the virtues of Nashville as a progressive, big-time city.

Near the end of August Schmittou sent the elaborate presentation, along with the required $100,000 application fee, to White's office.

He figures the Sounds invested some $200,000 in his efforts to sell Nashville to the major leagues.

"We had done all we could do," he says. "We had done our research and homework, proven we could sell tickets, and had everything in place to start building a new stadium. All we could do was wait."

Schmittou, along with Governor McWherter, Mayor Bill Boner, investor Reese Smith III, Chamber of Commerce official Mike Rollins, and others, flew to New York to present their case before the Expansion Committee.

"I thought we did a good job," says Schmittou, "especially compared with some other cities.

"An amusing thing happened when we left. Reese had hired a limo to carry us around, and when we got back to the airport he handed the driver a credit card. The driver said he had to have cash. We all began to go through our pockets and we found we had barely enough cash to pay the driver. We laughed about how there we were, ready to buy a $100 million baseball team, and we didn't have enough money to pay the limo driver."

Perhaps that was an omen, because the end of Schmittou's big-league dream came swiftly.

On December 18, 1990, the National League announced

its "short list" of six cities still in the running for an expansion team. Nashville wasn't on it. The cities still in contention were Buffalo; Denver; Miami; Orlando; Washington, D.C.; and St. Petersburg/Tampa.

White, in a short note to Schmittou, wrote:

"I regret to inform you that your group is not on the list."

Schmittou's $100,000 application fee was enclosed.

Nashville hadn't even made it to first base.

A shaken Schmittou called a press conference to make the announcement to the Nashville media and to express his consternation.

"Words cannot tell you how disappointed I am," he said, battling back tears as his voice quivered with emotion.

"This does not mean Nashville has done anything wrong; it means the National League has made the wrong decision.

"We were not selected, and for what earthly reason I don't know."

In a statement released from National League headquarters, Dallas Danforth, chairman of the NL Expansion Committee, termed the six finalists "The most qualified in terms of financial stability, significant community identification, and long-term commitment to a baseball club.

"The cities on the list are the best in terms of market size, government commitment to support baseball, and the stadium facilities in place or planned."

"That blew my mind," says Schmittou. "We were way ahead of some of the six in almost every category.

"It was very disappointing experience because I was confidant we would make the short list. But I'm not sorry I tried. Maybe we learned some things we can use next time—and I think there will be a next time. I still think Nashville is a major-league city.

"I will continue to try to get a major-league team. If I can't, then I will devote my efforts to building the best minor-league franchise in the country. That means we need a new stadium, not just to put us in contention for the next expansion in the year 2000 but in the meantime to keep pace in Class AAA."

Thus was launched yet another Schmittou battle—the fight for a new ball park—which would prove to be his toughest, most frustrating ever.

Schmittou had barely finished investing $5 million in his ball park when it "became obsolete."

"I guess it's kind of like when I won my last division and SEC crown at Vanderbilt in 1974," says Schmittou. "If I'd known that was going to be my last championship, an Vanderbilt, I think I'd have enjoyed it more when I had it.

"It's been sort of the same with the ball park. When we started doing our improvements, at that time we were the Cadillac of AA ball. Even when we went to AAA, with the exception of Louisville and Columbus, we pretty much had the nicest stadium in all AAA. Consequently, the players and the major-league clubs we were working with were tremendously happy.

"When our major-league drive came about, my only thought at the time was to do something that was feasible and not be an expensive program so that the club, over a period of time, could pay its own way and not be a burden on the taxpayers.

"Unbeknownst to me, even during the drive, the agreement the minor-leagues work under—the Professional Baseball Agreement—was getting renegotiated. At the end of 1989 and the beginning of 1990, the meetings between the major and minor leagues intensified.

"I paid very little attention at first, because throughout history there had never been a totally bitter dispute. But it began to become clear that this time was different. The major-league people, led by Eddie Einhorn and Bill Murray of the Commissioner's office, were determined to completely rewrite their relationship with the minor leagues.

"They wanted to change everything, from who paid what,

to the facilities their players played in. In July of 1990 they hit a total stalemate, with our agreement scheduled to end in four months.

"Finally, the president of the National Association, the governing body of the 17 minor leagues, asked me and five other minor-league owners to get involved with the negotiations and try to work something out.

"We met in Chicago and they presented a 200-page document asking the minor leagues to pay more money. The majors said they were spending more money on development and scouting, and some of the minors weren't paying much plus were selling their franchises for exorbitant amounts of money—all of which was true.

"They said all minor-league owners should pay more of the load and improve their ball parks to meet certain standards, if we wanted to keep doing business with them.

"I never suspected the impact the new Facilities Standards would have on minor-league baseball. As it turned out, it was positive for 95 percent of the clubs and cities involved, because they benefited from new or improved ball parks. Unfortunately, Nashville was in that other 5 percent.

"It would make it harder for me to operate, because I couldn't get a new stadium while everybody else was. The major element was that other teams were building newer, better facilities and we weren't. Of the eight teams in our league, five got totally new ball parks built.

"I don't fault our politicians for not understanding this, but I do fault them for not sitting down and trying to understand.

"In 1990, I still did not appreciate the impact. I was trying to get a new stadium built strictly to present for a major-league expansion team. I didn't realize I needed one just to keep pace with the rest of AAA baseball.

"Nashville's mayor at the time, Bill Boner, had been willing to work with us. He met with all his department heads—

water, sewer, zoning, and so on—and they all assured us they would work with us when we tried to get a stadium.

"Then the election was held and we had a new mayor, Phil Bredesen. It was stated to me at the time that promises had been made to the black community that a study would be made about getting Tennessee State University a new football stadium. The state had allocated $150,000 toward the study and Metro had matched it. So the mayor said he wanted to do that study first. He said that until the study was done, there would be no further discussion of a baseball stadium.

"A consulting firm from Atlanta did the study, and they rated eight or nine locations. They went to TSU and got their input as well. A year dragged on and finally the study came back. It recommended a parcel of land at Metro Center.

"I was caught cold on the Metro Center and probably made a mistake by not strongly objecting at the time. Maybe they read me as thinking I would go along with that site.

"But as one of our owners, Walter Nipper, pointed out, the site had been an old dump. Nobody wants to build a stadium on a landfill. So the consulting firm went back and found another site on a little island at Metro Center.

"I had already decided I wanted no part of Metro Center. Metro Center is perceived by many people, including me, as not being a very secure area. I also went out and studied traffic patterns and realized how hard it was to get off I-265 and over to the site.

"I talked to some of the TSU people and they weren't too high on the site either, for the same reasons.

"Plus, the fact of the matter is that a multipurpose stadium really doesn't fit either need. One sport or the other has to give. You either have to design a stadium with baseball sight lines, or vice-versa for football. TSU didn't want its football fans in an Atlanta stadium-type facility where the best seats are in the end zone, any more than I wanted my baseball fans sitting on the front row, 150 feet away from the playing field.

"We went to the meeting and one council member's only comment was, 'Where in the world are we going to find enough ball players to fill a major-league roster?'

"Another council member was only interested in TSU.

"We made our presentation, in which we said we would guarantee over $22 million to the city over 20 years if a stadium was built, but we had no interest in a Metro Center site. We explained why the perfect site would be at the intersection of I-24 and Briley Parkway.

"The committee in charge of studying the stadium proposal ended up making no recommendation.

"Really, neither party liked the idea—us or TSU—but since I opposed it, the way it came out was that Larry Schmittou had killed it."

Schmittou was not happy, but "at least no one had promised anything to anybody else. Then, about two or three months later, I read in the paper where the mayor is going to do a major project. We're going to build a $100 million downtown arena.

"Now, I personally thought Nashville needed both an arena and a stadium, but we shouldn't make the mistake we made with Municipal Auditorium, which was obsolete almost from the day it opened its doors.

"I considered then, and still do, the downtown location a bad site. Plus I thought the cost was way too high. If they were gong to spend $100 million, they could do what Kansas City did: put it somewhere else and build an arena, baseball stadium, and football stadium for the same amount of money.

"Someone asked my opinion, and even though a lot of people in the media and in the public think they should have an opinion and I shouldn't, I stated my thoughts on the matter. I've always been able to get the publicity, good or bad.

"When I said what I thought, the mayor didn't like it." And a feud began to fester between Schmittou and City hall.

"About six months after it was made clear to me that we weren't going to get a new ball park, other clubs were starting to make millions and millions of dollars of improvements at their stadiums.

"So now I'm getting complaints from the league president. Teams are coming in from state-of-the-art stadiums and when they get to Nashville they start complaining about how far behind we are. Bad locker rooms, no weight room, no batting cage. The fans aren't saying anything yet, but I realize parking is inadequate for large crowds, and if they have to park too far away, I worry about security. The neighborhood continues to deteriorate. Every day there is a new massage parlor springing up somewhere, or the homeless are moved closer to us.

"I'm not the smartest man in the world, but I'm also not the dumbest. I know two things: the mayor has no interest in a baseball stadium, and bonding is so important when you're spending $100 million and just gone up on taxes. The city has only so many dollars it can borrow. So it's going to be almost impossible to get a stadium."

The Sounds' working agreement with the Cincinnati Reds was about to expire, and Schmittou correctly guessed that they would choose to go with Indianapolis, which was closer and had a new stadium on the drawing board.

"I could see the writing on the wall," says Schmittou. "I knew we were going to lose that battle. I didn't know who we'd get. I wanted Cleveland, because they had the best prospects coming up. But Cleveland got a better deal with Charlotte, which had a new stadium.

"That left the Chicago White Sox, whose AAA team was in Vancouver. Chicago wanted to get closer to home and they were like us—they didn't have very many choices.

"We had some conversations and, without seeing our park, the White Sox agreed to come to Nashville. We signed with them and a couple of weeks later they came and looked at the ball park. One minute later they handed me a list of complaints. They start telling me all the things they didn't like—the field, the clubhouse, no weight room—which was all going to cost millions of dollars.

"I knew that what they were telling me was correct—that they had been in a nicer park the year before with their Class AA team in Birmingham—but I was still unprepared for it.

"What could I do? Call a press conference and explain what's going on? That makes the White Sox look bad, like they're coming in here complaining right away. It makes me and our ball club look bad, being so far behind other parks. It makes our fans start wondering, 'What's wrong with the stadium?' "

Schmittou decided to explore his options outside Davidson County.

"I thought we might go to one of the outlying counties—Rutherford, Wilson, or Williamson—while staying as close to Nashville as possible."

The mayor's position on Schmittou's threatened move was to wish him luck.

"As long as the Sounds stays in the Middle Tennessee region, I think that's 95 percent of the game," Bredesen said.

"If he (Schmittou) said he wanted to go to Cincinnati, I think we would try to break our backs to keep the Sounds here. But as long as he stays within the area and accessible to Nashvillians, I think it would be great if a surrounding county could help out with some of these capital needs of the region. Where Metro stands right now is, I would like to have a stadium. It's one of the facilities we need. But I don't have a feasible way of doing it yet."

So Schmittou began the process of trying to find a new home for the Sounds.

"I looked at some land in Lavergne, in Rutherford County," says Schmittou. "Then I looked at the Cool Springs site in Williamson. And at a site in Mount Juliet in Wilson."

After a year of probing and exploring, attending meetings, and making pitches to civic clubs in the various communities, none of the sites worked out. Snags were encountered at each location.

"It was a year of frustration," says Schmittou. "It was something I wish now I had not done. But you never know unless you try something.

"After all those efforts failed, I had one last approach. I studied what Oklahoma City did to get its stadium. The citizens voted for a temporary sales tax increase and in five years used it to pay for a baseball stadium and an arena, to remodel their fairgrounds and develop some other properties. At the end of five years the tax was rescinded.

"Since our mayor had the media and the Council locked up, I proposed that we let the people decide what they wanted to do. I asked the Council to pass a referendum to let the taxpayers vote on a one-quarter of one-cent tax increase, which would pay for a $40 million stadium in three years." We would then pay it back through our rent.

The referendum proposal failed to get through the Council by three votes.

"I was stunned," says Schmittou. "I couldn't believe that the Council would be so arrogant as to not even permit the taxpayers to vote on the proposal. But they didn't.

"So I'm at the end of my rope. I've tried everything I know to try and fought as hard as I can fight."

Less than a year later, the city would launch an effort to lure the Houston Oilers to Nashville. The proposed price tag, including the construction of a new, state-of-the-art football stadium: $300 million.

"It seems rather amazing that back then no one would consider $40 million for a baseball stadium but now we're willing to risk $300 million to build a stadium for a Texas millionaire," said Schmittou, referring to Oilers owner Bud Adams.

"Some narrow-minded members of the media would interpret this as if I am against any other professional sport coming to Nashville, which is absolutely not the case. I simply think that everyone should be willing to pay their fair share in the building of the stadium. We are proud of the fact that we built the citizens of Nashville a $12,000,000 million stadium without using one cent of Metro taxpayer money."

CHAPTER IX
GETTING INK

"You owe nothing to the media other than the truth."

L arry Schmittou says the perception that he carries a run
ning feud with the media is inaccurate.

"I think you can narrow it down to a small few," he says.

But, admits Schmittou, he often questions how the media
goes about covering sports nowadays.

"I grew up in a time when the only media story was about
the game or the players," he says. "That's changed. The media
now thinks they ought to be able to tell you how to run your
business, how to run your life.

"But if you ever suggest to them how to do something,
you're a sorry so and so.

"I've always been a person to tell it like it is, and some
people have a problem with that. My problem with the media,
99 percent of it, is those people who call themselves colum-
nists. I personally think they're the ones who weren't good
enough to be able to cover a team on a day-to-day basis, so the
newspaper made them a columnist. I've never had a problem
with a beat writer."

Schmittou went so far as to ban Joe Biddle, a columnist with *The Nashville Banner*, from the Sounds press box in 1994.

"It all started years before when Biddle walked in one day and wanted to tell me how to count my attendance," says Schmittou. "We count tickets sold, and so on a buyout night if we wanted to count 50,000 people, under the criteria we use, we could do it.

"I don't tell the newspapers how to count their circulation. If the *Tennessean* sells 240,000 papers on Sunday, does that mean all 240,000 got read?

"They don't have to report the attendance in the paper if they don't want to, but they aren't going to tell me how to count it."

Schmittou claims Biddle later "wrote a couple of cheap shots, making fun of people. I don't like the style of people who try to belittle others. I don't care for that. One thing led to another."

The clincher was a column Biddle wrote expressing an opinion that Schmittou treated some of his employees—including some family members—shabbily. He questioned how Greer Stadium was being run and maintained. The criticism came on the very day that all Class AAA executives arrived in Nashville for the association's All-Star game.

Schmittou hit the proverbial ceiling when he read the stinging critique and immediately informed Biddle that his presence was no longer welcome at Greer Stadium.

"I don't care what shots the media takes at me personally," says Schmittou. "But I won't stand by and let anyone take shots at my family or my ball club when what they say isn't true.

"What Biddle wrote wasn't accurate and I told him I didn't appreciate it. If he felt that way, he could just stay away."

Near the start of the 1995 season, Schmittou says he received a half-hearted letter of apology from Biddle, which he refused to accept.

"I informed Biddle that I expected him to print his apology in the Banner and to give it the same play he had given that column," says Schmittou. "I never heard back from him.

"I figure he just wanted to come back because at the time it looked like Michael Jordan was going to be playing for us, and Biddle didn't want to miss a national story like that. When Jordan didn't show, I guess Biddle lost interest. That suited me just fine."

Schmittou continues to allow other *Banner* writers access to the press box, and the afternoon paper's coverage of the Sounds has not been affected.

"I have no quarrel with the *Banner*," says Schmittou. "My quarrel was with Biddle. And actually, I think Joe works harder than any other writer in Nashville and is very knowledgeable on all sports. I think he has improved since I wrote him and his editor."

Schmittou doesn't play favorites—or unfavorites—with the two Nashville newspapers; he also took to task David Climer, a writer for the *Tennessean*, on more than one occasion.

Michael Jordan was visiting Greer Stadium as a member of the Birmingham Barons in the summer of 1994, when a young fan dashed onto the field and rushed toward the superstar. A Sounds official tackled the intruder, and Climer, who was covering the game, wrote that the employee used undue force in subduing the young trespasser.

Schmittou was furious.

"What did Climer expect our security man to do? Stand back and wait to see what happened? What if he had run up to Jordan and attacked him, or injured him in some way? The employee reacted exactly as he should have reacted under the circumstances. I thought Climer took a cheap shot and made a hero out of someone who had run 300 feet while being told about 10 times to get back in the stands. To me that was clearly a case of yellow journalism."

Schmittou and Climer would exchange other personal barbs later on. Climer suggested in a column that Schmittou was less than truthful when he claimed that he could secure a Canadian Football League team for the city if it built a multipurpose stadium.

"I resent being called a liar in print by David Climer," said Schmittou in a scathing letter to the editor. "If he had bothered to call the CFL—or even check with me—he would have learned that what I said was true. For $3 million I could have gotten a CFL franchise. I didn't want to run it—I would have sold it to someone else—but the fact is, I could have gotten one, just as I said. I didn't lie."

Schmittou once canceled his subscription to the *Tennessean* because he felt the paper was not devoting fair and sufficient coverage to the Sounds.

He also lambasted the *Banner* for a front-page "expose" of an audit during the Sounds' formative years. A team of auditors found no wrong-doing and Schmittou received an apology.

In the spring of 1991 Schmittou said he hoped a local cable TV company would not carry Cincinnati Reds games and, in fact, said he would prefer to see all major-league telecasts blacked out in Tennessee. He noted that such a decision would not be his, but major-league baseball's.

John Bibb, at the time the sports editor of the *Tennessean* and a long-time personal friend of Schmittou, chastised the Sounds owners for "being out of line."

"He has definitely strayed from the basepaths," wrote the normally mild-mannered Bibb. "He isn't looking where he's running. Schmittou calculates he loses attendance every time a major-league game is telecast in Tennessee. That may or may not be true, but his preference for a statewide blackout of baseball telecast is unreasonable."

Schmittou didn't blink or budge

"I stand by what I said," he says, in response to Bibb's criticism, adding, "I know John never bought a ticket anyway."

"Obviously, I don't run baseball, but I do run the Nashville Sounds, and I see any baseball telecast as competition. I'll say it again: I don't believe I'm out of line when I say I'd prefer no TV games in Tennessee, just as I'm sure the morning paper would prefer not to have an evening paper to compete with."

Schmittou took an equally hard-line stand in opposition to an effort to bring a World League of American Football (WLAF) team to Nashville in 1989. He felt the NFL-backed spring football league would compete with the Sounds for fans and media attention. He predicted that if it came, it would not be successful.

"I've been honest and up-front from the start," said Schmittou at the time. "I'm completely opposed to Nashville getting one of those teams. I respect the individuals involved, but I'd feel the same way if it were my brother."

"I'm not worried about going up against it five days (the WLAF's proposed home schedule); but if Nashville ends up with a team, I'll see to it there are a million free Sounds tickets out each time they play.

"What concerns me most is the year-round competition for media coverage. This morning's paper had a top-of-the page headline on a team we don't have and a bottom-of-the-page headline on a team we do have (the Sounds).

"I don't care what they call it, it's still minor-league football and I don't see that as a big boost for our city."

"I honestly can't believe he means what he's been saying," said Charles Harris, one of the potential WLAF investors. "I can't believe he would deny Nashville and Middle Tennessee the opportunity to enjoy pro football."

"That's vintage Schmittou," said former mayor Richard Fulton, who represented Tennessee Pro Football Inc. in the WLAF talks. "Larry won't be happy until they close all the theaters on the nights the Sounds are playing."

Schmittou counter-punched, saying, "I find all this puzzling, considering Fulton's noninvolvement in sports while he was mayor."

As it turned out, it was all a moot argument; Vanderbilt University, which had the city's only acceptable football stadium, elected not to lease it to the WLAF and Nashville's hopes of getting a team vanished. The WLAF eventually folded.

"Charlie Harris and his investors should thank me," says Schmittou. "I saved them a lot of money, maybe millions of dollars."

Two years later the WLAF quietly folded its tents.

"I'd like to get credit when I'm right about something," says Schmittou, "and I told people it wouldn't work. There's never been a case of a sport playing outside its natural session and being a success. I knew summertime football wouldn't go over."

Schmittou's stand against pro football was consistent with his opposition to a horse-racing track in 1987. He joined forces with an antigambling group and donated $5,000 to the political action committee to help defeat the racetrack proposal.

"It has nothing to do with the moral issue," said Schmittou. "I'd be battling the track for the entertainment dollar and media space. If it costs us one fan or one inch of space in the newspapers, it would hurt the Sounds. I've never seen a horse race, but I'm convinced a track here would not be good for the Sounds.

"I was very much in favor of the citizens having a right to vote on this, and of course it was defeated not once, but twice. Now, 10 years later, there still is no track in Tennessee. Could I have been right?"

Schmittou can't understand why the media continually takes him to task for opposing other pro sports in Nashville.

"The two papers oppose each other every day," he says. "They compete against each other for stories and for readers. If one paper gets a story about a football signee, the other paper virtually ignores it.

"The very things I get criticized for—ignoring the competition and going for the jugular—I learned from newspapers.

"Every media outlet wants to get the story first. If you give the story to one paper, it loves you, and the other paper crucifies you. I've learned that over the years.

"I've never claimed to try to please the media. In the first place, how many of them buy a ticket to a game?

"I try to please those fans who buy tickets and sit down in the seats. I go down and meet them, and their opinion matters to me. Some sportswriter, who only gets half the facts right and who never buys a ticket—well, his opinion really doesn't concern me.

"A guy who comes in on a free ticket, parks free, then criticizes me—to heck with that guy!"

CHAPTER X
FAMILY MATTERS

*"The most important job in life is to be
a good husband or wife and parent."*

Larry Schmittou says that as a youngster he was too involved in sports and too busy with the family farm to pay much attention to girls—until a petite classmate named Shirley Reynolds invited him to go on a church hayride.

"Shirley and I went to school together at Cohn High," says Schmittou. "For our first three years I guess we knew who each other was, but that was about the extent of it. I didn't go to parties and socialize a lot. It wasn't until our senior year, when we had a sociology class together, that we really became acquainted.

"She had just broken up with a member of the football team, and I think she was kinda looking around for a replacement when she asked me if I'd like to go on the hayride with her."

Shirley's version:

"First of all, it happened during our junior year, not our senior year," she says. "And Larry wasn't nearly as shy as he lets on; I remember a certain little red-haired cheerleader he paid a lot of attention to. But yes, the rest is pretty accurate: I asked him out and we kept going together after that."

What was Schmittou's attraction?

"He was just sweet and nice to me," says Shirley. "I don't know exactly what it was about him, other than that. He just seemed different from all the other boys."

Schmittou was not sure his extremely protective mother would permit him to go on the hayride, "but when I asked her she said I could go. I guess she figured that I was old enough to learn about the opposite sex.

"So Shirley and I went on the hayride together—this was along in September—and we continued to date on and off the rest of the school term. Most of our dates consisted of going to a ball game, then going over to Shirley's parents house for popcorn and sodas.

"The only problem with that was that it was three miles from my house to Shirley's, and I didn't have a car. I had to walk. I'd always stay to the last possible minute, then run to make it home by the exact moment my mother had ordered me to be home. With all that running, I was in better shape than the guys on the track team.

"I got to meet a lot of neighborhood dogs on a personal basis, as they chased me home in the dark. I guess all that running I did between Shirley's house and mine was the best training I ever had."

When Christmas rolled around, Schmittou realized he had to get a gift for his new girlfriend.

"Not having any experience at things like that—and also not having any money—I wrapped an old radio I had and gave it to Shirley for Christmas. I could tell she wasn't all that thrilled, getting a used radio for Christmas, but I figured it was the thought that counted."

"Yes, I remember that radio," says Shirley. "But the gift I remember most was a little rhinestone pin Larry gave me the first Christmas we were married. I know it didn't cost much, because we didn't have much money, but it meant the world to me. I still have it."

Schmittou grew fond of Shirley's parents, Harvey and Rachel Reynolds, "and I guess they liked me; they never told me to stay away from their daughter, and I took that as a good sign."

There was just one hitch with the budding romance:

"My mother was a devout Baptist, and Shirley and her parents were devout Church of Christ members," says Schmittou. "But somehow we survived all that and continued to date on through the summer."

"Mrs. Schmittou was a wonderful lady," recalls Shirley. "But she was very set in her ways when it came to religion. I remember she once wrote a letter to the editor in the Tennessean, giving us Camolites down-the-road.

"But I came to respect her beliefs and admired her very much. We became really close after Larry and I married. I thought the world of her."

When they married, Schmittou joined the Church of Christ in deference to his bride's wishes. Later, after their children were grown, he returned to his original Baptist faith, "where I'd always been, deep down. I hardly ever miss a Reverend Bill Sherman sermon on TV."

Despite their differences in religion, Janie Schmittou and Shirley's mother, Rachel, also became good friends.

"I think they both respected each other for their deep convictions," says Schmittou, "even though they didn't see eye-to-eye."

The Reynolds family "was totally like my family to a degree—hard-working, close, and caring—and totally opposite in some other ways," says Schmittou.

"Shirley came from a small family; she had one younger sister, Betty. They lived on Nebraska Avenue, and people in my neighborhood thought all the people in her neighborhood were rich. They all had nice houses and owned cars.

"Of course as I grew older I realized they were not rich by any means; they were middle-class. But by our standards in my neighborhood at the time, they seemed rich."

Harvey Reynolds owned a feed store on Charlotte Avenue.

"We raised pigs and hogs, and my father bought feed from Shirley's father," says Schmittou. "The first time I recall meeting Mr. Reynolds he was holding a contest to name two pigs. My dad named one Ike, after Eisenhower, and he won one of the pigs."

In the fall of 1958 Schmittou entered Peabody College, and Shirley enrolled at Lipscomb College and they began to go steady.

"I don't know how they do it today, but back then we swapped class rings," says Schmittou. "When you did that, you knew it was serious. A little while after that, we decided to get married."

The wedding was held in November 1959.

"I remember there was a very exciting Vanderbilt-Tennessee football game that day," says Schmittou. My best man and I listened to the end of the game at church, before the wedding. Vandy beat the Vols 14–0 in Knoxville. It was a great day.

"We got married on a Saturday, and I had to go back to work at the Ford Glass Plant on Sunday. We had to postpone our honeymoon awhile."

Shirley took it all in stride.

"She couldn't have been more understanding and supportive in anything I wanted to do," says Schmittou. "She was always interested in what I was doing, whether it was playing or coaching."

Shirley left college after two years to, in Schmittou's words, "go to work and help me fulfill my dreams." She took a job in the psychiatric unit of Vanderbilt Children's Hospital.

"We didn't see much of each other during that time," says

Schmittou. "I was working at Ford, going to college, and coaching baseball.

"I don't know how she put up with me through that period of my life, because I was very impatient. I was just learning to coach on a competitive level and really put my personal goals totally ahead of everything else, including my wife. Until I got out of college and settled down a little bit, we were going in opposite directions a lot of the time."

"I don't remember it that way at all," says Shirley. "I understood how determined Larry was to succeed. He was working a lot of long, hard hours, but I never felt neglected. I went to all his games and we spent as much time together as our schedules would permit.

"What I remember most is that we were going through some difficult financial times back then, as most young couples do, and we were both working awfully hard to make ends meet."

Throughout her marriage, Shirley has backed her husband's every career move and decision.

"When I first got out of college I had a job feeler from El Dorado High School in Illinois," says Schmittou. "Shirley and I went to check it out. It was a nice little school, but in a hick town. They had an oil pump across the street from the school.

"I could tell by the way Shirley looked that she wasn't crazy about it. And neither was I. So we came back home."

Years later, when Schmittou got a job offer to join the Texas Rangers as a front-office executive, the only person he consulted was his wife.

"I called Shirley and told her I had the offer and it was something I thought I'd like to try. She said, 'Fine. When do we leave?'

"That was the only comment she made. On the spur of the moment she had to get ready to pack up and move our family from Nashville to Texas, and she never hesitated one second."

Shirley gave up her job when her children began to arrive: Debbie (now 31), Ronnie (29), Mike (28), Susan (27), and Steve

(22).

When her last child, Steve, reached toddler stage, Shirley began operating a day-care center out of her home. Shortly afterward, her husband built a ball park, founded the Nashville Sounds, and again she changed occupations to help fill his needs.

"Since we had absolutely no money, our entire family had to pitch in and help out," says Schmittou. "Shirley started out working in concessions, then helped in souvenirs, did the payroll, sold tickets, answered the phone—she did whatever needed doing at the time."

As the franchise grew and the staff expanded, Shirley was able to devote less time to the ball club and more time to her own interests—working with her church, tending the sick and elderly.

"I'm still very active and involved with the club," she says. "I work now because I enjoy it, not because I have to. But the thing I love most of all is being a mother and a grandmother—I consider that my real 'occupation.' "

All the Schmittou children played an active role in the ball club, starting at ground-level jobs.

"I made sure they didn't start out with a high salary, a title, a cushy job," says Schmittou. "I wanted them to start out just like any other employee and work their way up. I tried to never give my kids special treatment.

"Mike, who was about 10 when he started, was my Snow-Cone director," chuckles Schmittou. "Debbie made pizzas. Ronnie worked in concessions and souvenirs. Susan kinda helped out wherever she was needed. Steve was too young to do much; he just hung around. When he got older, he pitched in and did what the other kids had been doing. Mike and Ronnie also both served as bat boys and worked on the grounds crew."

After graduating from David Lipscomb University, Debbie later worked her way up to business manager, handling those duties while Schmittou was away at Texas. She continued the duties until she got married and began devoting her time to her teaching career.

After she graduated from David Lipscomb University, Susan took over the full-time business duties and remained in the position until she got married and opted for motherhood.

Ronnie, meanwhile, graduated from Texas A&M, where he had enrolled while the family was living in Texas, and returned home to help run the family business. He assumed the director of concessions position for two years, then became marketing and business manager. Mike, after graduating from Tennessee Tech, became director of merchandising and assistant concessions manager.

Schmittou says being father and boss to his children "was both good and bad. In the long run, I think it was positive. I always knew I could count on them because they had a personal stake in the business. I knew they would devote the time and effort and desire.

"But there was a hard part, too. It's so hard to treat your own children as just regular employees. I'd seen the same thing when a coach would try to coach his own kids on a ball team. He tends to either be too hard or too easy on them. It's hard to be neutral.

"In the long run you get closer to them. When they get older they will look back and hopefully appreciate what you tried to do—correct them when they needed correcting and so on. But at the time it can be hard. Their feelings get hurt a little quicker and stay hurt a little longer when it's their own father getting on them."

For example, Schmittou once fired his daughter Susan.

"She had just gotten out of high school and was immature," says Schmittou. "She loved being with her friends, which is understandable for an 18-year-old. But I tried to explain that she also had certain duties and obligations if she was going to hold down a job.

"She had worked for two weeks, quit, and went to do something else. Then she came back and was working at the third-base ticket gate. One night I went out and saw Debbie working the booth. I said, 'Where's Susan?'

"Debbie said, 'Oh, she'll be back in a minute.'

"I let it go, but at the end of the night I went back and said, 'OK, where's Susan?'

"Turned out she had gone off snow skiing with some of her buddies to Colorado. So I fired her—the same as I'd fire any other employee who'd told me they were going to work and didn't show up.

"I learned to separate my children from my employees. When they come through that door, they're employees first and my children second. Right or wrong, that's the way I feel.

"Susan knew she'd done wrong. She pouted around awhile but eventually she came over and asked for a job. She was in college and wanted to work at a Rivergate Mall gift shop Walter Nipper and I had just opened.

"I basically told her, 'This is your last go-around with me. If you don't show up, you're history. This is your last job with me.'

"I think that was her maturing point. It helped her grow up. She was loyal, hard-working and came from the gift shop back to the Sounds as business manager. She did a great job during some of our toughest times. I'm proud of her."

Susan says she doubts that her father realized how terribly hurt she was at being fired.

"I was going through a very difficult time right then," she says. "We had just moved back to Nashville from Texas and I'd left all my friends behind. I was trying to make new friends and that's one reason I really wanted to go on that church retreat.

"I'd been working hard and it was just for one night. I couldn't see why it would hurt for me to miss one day's work. Even though I had made arrangements for someone to work for me, I guess my mistake was not telling my dad, and just taking off. But when he fired me, it really hurt my feelings.

Above: Greer Stadium rose from humble beginnings in 1978, but it didn't take long for a line to form at Schmittou's executive office."

Right: The Sounds were a family affair from the start. Here Schmittou and wife Shirley pose with children Ronnie and Debbie (back row), and Susan, Mike, and Steve.

Left: Schmittou and the Sounds' first manager, Chuck Goggin, in the dugout with celebrity investor Jerry Reed and Southern League president Billy Hitchcock, on Opening Night 1978.

Schmittou and Jerry Reed chat with agent Harry Warner, while popular Nashvill radio/TV person-ality Ralph Emery waits in the background.

Schmittou has reason to smile; his growing Nashville Sounds smashed minor league attendance records in 1990.

Schmittou meets with baseball immortal Henry Aaron and Atlanta Braves traveling secretary Donald Davidson during *The Nashville Banner*'s Banquet of Champions.

Schmittou credits the late Conway Twitty (left), his first major investor, with helping to get the Sounds off the ground. Conway is joined by fellow stars Tennessee Ernie Ford and Charlie McCoy.

Hall of Famer Ernie Banks and Phil Niekro came to town in 1977 to help Schmittou drum up baseball interest.

Some of baseball's biggest names gathered at Greer Stadium over the years. Here Schmittou welcomes (l to r) New York Yankees owner George Steinbrenner, Whitey Ford, Bill White, Mickey Vernon, and Bill Bergesch.

Schmittou signs a working agreement with the New York Yankees.

The winner of the "Annie Contest," Ann Quillen, is surrounded by the Schmittou clan: Shirley, Debbie, Larry, Susan, Mike, Ron, and Steve.

Schmittou, who left Nashville briefly to serve as an executive with the Texas Rangers, relaxes in his Texas Stadium office in 1984.

Schmittou is always ready to lend a hand to civic causes. Here he and his wife, Shirley, join Christie Hauck for a pasta judging contest to benefit the Vanderbilt Nursing School.

One of country music's biggest stars, Loretta Lynn, takes in a Sounds game with Schmittou and music promoter Snuffy Miller.

Schmittou welcomes celebrities to the 1983 Baseball Winter Meetings (l to r): Bob Smith, Jerry Reed, former Commissioner Happy Chandler, former Governor Lamar Alexander, Schmittou, and then-Commissioner Bowie Kuhn.

Country music singer George Strait, left, and Roger Clemens visit the Texas Rangers locker room. Strait had just finished a stadium concert, following a game in which Clemens had taken a no-hitter into the 9th inning.

More notables visit the clubhouse: back row, l to r, are Gene Smith, Steve Smith, Reese Smith Jr., Reese Smith III, Richard Sterban, Farrell Owens, and Schmittou; middle row: Roy Carter, Billy Griggs, Bob Elliott, Walter Nipper, Jimmy Miller, Lynn Greer; front row: Jack Butterfield, Whitey Ford, George Steinbrenner, Gov. Lamar Alexander, Mickey Mantle and Bill Bergesch.

The Oak Ridge Boys take in a game at Greer Stadium. Richard Sterban (left) was one of the Sounds' early investors.

Schmittou wasn't too busy with baseball to give away his daughter Debbie in marriage.

Even as an owner, Schmittou still draws on his coaching days to offer a few batting tips.

Flanked by then-Governor Ned McWherter, Mayor Bill Boner, and Vanderbilt Vice-Chancellor Bill Jenkins, Schmittou makes his 1990 pitch for a National League franchise.

Schmittou entertains family, friends, and Sounds employees in Las Vegas during the Class AAA All-Star Game.

Whitey Ford, Richard Sterban, and Mickey Mantle enjoy a clubhouse chat in 1980.

Pete Rose, as manager of the Cincinnati Reds, was a frequent Greer Stadium visitor. Here he talks with Schmittou and former Sounds business manager George Dyce.

"When I came back to work full-time, sometimes he would yell at us in public and it was really embarrassing. Sometimes I'd get so mad that when I would get home I'd immediately go grab the newspaper and start looking through the classifieds, determined to get another job.

"But I loved working at the ball park. I liked baseball and I liked my job. It was just hard sometimes, working for my dad. But the day I quit for good, I broke into tears."

The reason she quit was to devote full time to her own children.

"I had made up my mind I was always going to put my kids first," she says. "I don't know if part of that feeling came from my own experience or not, but as a little girl I would go to spend the night with my friends and I'd see how much time their fathers spent with them. I was amazed. I wondered why my dad didn't spend that much time with me.

"I especially remember a big doll house one of my friends had. She said her father made it for her. I thought 'Why didn't my dad ever make me one?' Growing up, I didn't have a father in that same way. He was always so busy."

In retrospect, Susan understands the lessons her father was trying to instill in his children.

"I admire him now," she says. "I've learned a lot about how his family struggled when he was growing up, and I know what a strong work ethic he has. He worked hard and he wanted his kids to work hard. He wanted to teach us values.

"But as a little girl and later as a teenager, it was hard to understand some of the things he did. We had to work when other kids our age didn't. I realize now he was just doing what he thought was best for us, and I appreciate it."

"He was always tough on us," says Ronnie. "I know Susan's feelings were hurt when Dad fired her, and I guess there were some tensions over it, but every family has tensions. When you work together those tensions probably become greater.

"He was hard on me, but I was even harder on myself. I

felt like I had the best job a kid could have. I got to be bat boy, I got to hang around the clubhouse with the players . . . for a kid who loved baseball, it was great.

"I've always liked being around my dad and watching him work. I try to listen to what he says and learn how he responds to people.

"He's always been in the papers one way or another, and that's part of the job, making sure the people of Nashville know him—whether they like him or dislike him.

"Sometimes I want to say, 'Why did you have to say anything?' But then I realize that's just him."

Mike says being the son and employee of Larry Schmittou "has always been neat. I enjoyed it. Sometimes at school someone would ask me, 'Are you related to the man who owns the baseball team?' And I'd feel proud.

"One thing I always thought was kinda funny: People seemed to think that because dad owned the Sounds we were rich or some sort of big shots. Nothing could be further from the truth. We always lived in a simple house and drove an older-model car. My dad never threw money at us kids; he put most of what he made back into the team.

"At times I think he expects more from us than he does the other employees. I work hard to please him, because he always gives 100 percent and I want to do the same."

Mike says the criticism his father often attracts "gets to me sometimes. I want to defend him because he's my dad, but his advice is to just let it slide off. It's frustrating to hear people criticize him after all the good things he's done for this city. He's like any other businessman—he tries to do what's best for his business, which is baseball, and I don't see why people can't understand that.

"I don't think many people really know him. He's a great person and a great father."

"He is a good dad," says Debbie Schmittou Algood. "When we

were working for him he was harder on us than the rest of his employees, but he was teaching us a good work ethic. He tried his best.

"My relationship with my dad has gotten closer as I've grown older. I appreciate him more."

Steve Schmittou, the youngest member of the clan, admits he is also the "most rebellious."

Like his older sister Susan, Steve says he often wondered why his father didn't spend more time with him.

"I had a good friend who played sports and his father always seemed to be at his games," recalls Steve. "I missed that."

Steve says he is not interested in joining the Sounds family.

"I love baseball, love going to the park," he says, "but I don't care for the business part. It's just not my cup of tea. I don't know if it's because I grew up in it or what, but I just don't see myself working in baseball."

Steve says he understands some of the hard lessons his father tried to teach his children.

"He's not mean or anything like that," he says. "He's just honest. He tells you straight-out what he thinks and sometimes that hurts people's feelings. But he always had time to sit down and talk to me whenever I came to him with something. I just wish we'd had more time together.

"Now my dad makes a lot of time for his grandchildren, and I wonder if that's because of some of the time he missed with his own kids. But I understand the things he was busy with, and I know he wasn't absent because he didn't care about us.

"He's a great dad."

Shirley never shared her husband's philosophy that once the Schmittou brood reported to work they became employees first, her children second.

"No," she says. "They were always my children, first and foremost. And they always will be.

"I thought Larry was too hard on them at times. I understood what he was trying to do—not play favorites with his children in front of the other employees—but that's hard to do as far as I'm concerned."

At times the Schmittou children confided in their mother and, admits Shirley, "I didn't always tell Larry what they were thinking, or how they felt. He could be their boss, but I was still their mother. I never interfered with anything he tried to do, but my children always knew they could come to me if they had a question or problem."

Shirley has always been her husband's staunchest defender.

"Larry tries not to let things get to him, but it always makes me mad to read or hear things people say about him," she says. "Especially when I know they're not true.

"Not a whole lot of people really know the Larry Schmittou I've known for so many years. He's such a good person and done so many good things for people that most folks never know about—probably including me."

Shirley says she has enjoyed going through life as Mrs. Larry Schmittou.

"If I could go back and do it all over again, I wouldn't change a thing," she says. "We've been through some hard times together and some good times together, and even the hard times weren't all that terrible, looking back—they helped bring us closer because we got through them together.

"One thing I have to say about being married to Larry: Life is never boring."

"I've been blessed all my life, being able to do the exact job I wanted to work at, with a wife of 36 years at my side," says Schmittou. "And also five wonderful children who have prepared themselves educationally and are becoming good citizens.

"I tried to raise my kids a lot like I had been raised and teach them the importance of a good work ethic and to respect their elders. And I stressed the value of a good education.

"I love them very much. Sometimes the hardest thing to do is love your kids and also at the same time be firm with them.

"I wish there were certain things I could have done, but you have to make decisions at specific times during your life. My job as a baseball coach and football recruiter, for example, required me to be on the road a lot. I made every effort to be with them as much as I possibly could. A lot of times I'd take the family with me on baseball trips, and in the summer we would visit various teams together.

"Once we went to New York to see the Yankees, and George Steinbrenner invited us all up to his personal box. Steve, my youngest son, had a loose tooth at the time and was horsing around and knocked it out. Everybody in the booth—the family, George, and several of his important guests—stopped watching the game and started helping look for Steve's tooth so he could stick it under his pillow for the tooth fairy.

"Looking back, we had some fun times together."

Chapter XI
Baseball Buddies

"Make friendship a fine art."

For Larry Schmittou, much of the fun and fascination of baseball comes from the people and personalities in baseball.

Over the years he has rubbed shoulders with the game's nobility—its biggest names and most famous figures—as well as with a colorful ensemble of delightful unknowns.

One of Schmittou's favorite players was Mickey Mantle, the magnificent Yankees slugger whose personal life tragically deteriorated.

After undergoing a transplant to replace a liver ravaged by decades of alcohol abuse, a frail Mantle stood before the nation and pleaded with youngsters, "Don't do what I did." He died shortly afterward.

"I grew up worshipping Mickey Mantle," says Schmittou. "The best investment I ever made involved Mantle. When I was a kid, my dad worked in a grocery store and I started collecting baseball cards. They were a penny apiece. The ones I collected of Mantle for a penny each in 1952 are now worth at least $7,500. I've never sold one.

"The first major-league baseball game I ever saw was in Detroit with my uncle, on a night when the Tigers were playing the Yankees. The day before, Mickey had hit a home run out of Tiger Stadium. The night we were there he hit a home run on the roof on his first time up, and at his next at-bat he hit one right to our feet in the leftfield upper deck.

"There must have been 50 fans who ran out onto the field to try to touch him as he ran the bases. They had to turn on the fire hoses to get the people off the field so play could resume. Talk about a kid from Nashville being impressed.

"In later years, after I became involved with professional baseball, I got to know Mantle very well. When the Sounds were with the Yankees, George Steinbrenner did many things for Nashville, including bringing a lot of past and present Yankee stars to town, including Mantle.

"I remember most vividly one time, around 1982, Bill Garrett asked me to get a speaker to roast to raise money for a cornea transplant center. I arranged to get Steinbrenner to come down to be roasted. He also brought Whitey Ford, Marv Throneberry, Phil Rizzuto, Roger Merrill, and Mantle.

"I sat next to Mickey that night and he'd had a couple of drinks. He was rather abusive to a fan who had asked for an autograph, got one, then came back and wanted another. That was the first time I'd seen that side of Mantle. He had been drinking, and I think he'd be the first to tell you that's what caused most of his problems.

"Otherwise, he was always such a charming guy. We had him here several times to meet with our owners. He loved to talk baseball. When I went with the Rangers, Mantle was one of nine Yankees broadcasters and sometimes when they'd come in for a game he and I would sit up on the roof, where it wasn't so crowded, and just talk baseball. How I cherish these moments.

"One day he came into the stadium club for a drink before a game. Some player had just signed for $1 million and someone asked Mickey, 'How much would you be worth, if you played today?'

"Mantle told us a story: 'The year I won the Triple Crown I had a $65,000 contract. The next season I had better stats but didn't win the Triple Crown, and the club offered me $5,000 less than I'd made the year before. I complained and wound up making the same salary—$65,000—after back-to-back great seasons.

'If I played today and put up those numbers, when I'd see Mr. Steinbrenner, I'd just say, "Hello, partner."'

"He had that kind of sense of humor and was a great story teller. He was a wonderful guy to be around, except, I understand, when he had too much to drink.

"I didn't see many of those dark sides. I visited him at his restaurant in New York City once and he was as gracious and nice as he could be.

"It was really tragic, the things that happened to him . . . his knees going bad, losing his son, his battle with alcohol. Mickey played baseball in Oklahoma with Bill Pace, my athletic director at Vanderbilt, and Pace told me Mantle once told him he always thought he'd die young because none of the men in his family had lived very long. I've always wondered if that was why he didn't take better care of himself.

"But he was a great player and he's still a hero even though he made mistakes, as we all have. You have to admire him for coming forward at that stage of his life and being big enough to admit his mistakes and warn little kids to avoid some of the things he did—don't burn the candle at both ends, thinking your career will never end.

"I was a Mickey Mantle fan as a kid, and I'm still a Mickey Mantle fan."

Then there is Steinbrenner himself, the oft-maligned Yankees owner who is frequently chastised for his heavy-handed management style.

"I cannot say anything but good things about George

Steinbrenner," says Schmittou.

"Remember the roast Steinbrenner attended to help raise money for a cornea transplant center here? It was a $100-a-plate dinner and raised a lot of money. What we lacked, Steinbrenner contributed—over $40,000—and today we have the Joan Steinbrenner Cornea Transplant Center at Vanderbilt.

"When I formed the Sounds, our mayor, Richard Fulton, wanted us to sign with the Yankees because of Steinbrenner's connection with the Nashville Bridge Company. But I'd already committed to the Reds, because I originally hoped to get a Class AAA franchise.

"After two years with the Reds, I decided to leave because the Reds would not permit us to use a designated hitter even though the other teams did. I am not a fan of the DH, but if the other team is using it and we aren't, our chances of winning go down, and I don't think that's fair."

Schmittou called the Yankees and said he wanted to sign with their organization.

"They were all for it, so after we got everything worked out, I said, 'How about having a little press conference down here?'

"Next day Steinbrenner, Whitey Ford, and Mickey Mantle all showed up. It was like that during our entire association with the Yankees. Anything I asked for, any favor I needed, Steinbrenner was willing to grant. He really wanted to be in Nashville. The Yankees and Sounds were a perfect match.

"He wanted to put a good team on the field—George is very competitive—and he did. The first year we had Steve (bye-bye) Balboni and made the playoffs.

"I invited Steinbrenner to come to speak to our Old Timers banquet. Jeff Lavander, Jack Lavander's son, was at the door that night when Steinbrenner came in. Jeff said 'Yes sir' to him and that seemed to impress him. I guess kids in New York don't say 'Yes sir.'

"Then he noticed Joe 'Black Cat' Reiley standing to one side. Black Cat was wearing a Yankees jacket and cap. That really seemed to impress Steinbrenner.

"So when he finally got up to speak, he had a five-page speech prepared, but he totally disregarded it. He began to speak on manners and loyalty. He had been inspired by Jeff Lavander's politeness and Black Cat's Yankees outfit.

"He had asked me who Black Cat was, and I told him he was famous on the sandlot circuit as a bat boy. He also believed he could put a hex on the opposing team.

"In his speech, Steinbrenner referred to him as 'Blackie, a young man of great loyalty,' not realizing that Black Cat was about 15 years older than George, and that if the speaker had been from Seattle, Black Cat would have showed up wearing a Mariners jacket and cap.

"George always remembered Black Cat. He sends him a Christmas present every year, and one spring when I was with the Rangers we were at spring training in Pompano Beach, Florida, playing the Yankees and I saw Black Cat. He was wearing a Yankees uniform, standing next to Billy Martin, as the team's bat boy.

"Black Cat had told Steinbrenner that his dream was to be a Yankees bat boy, and George granted his wish.

"Today Black Cat still sells souvenirs at Sounds games, at least when he's not in Florida with his personal friend, George Steinbrenner."

Schmittou recounts numerous instances of Steinbrenner's generosity.

"He learned that Jack Lavander was building a youth baseball park in Twitty City and donated $5,000 to it. He asked what he could do for Vanderbilt and ended up giving the athletic department $10,000.

"One morning my phone rang and rang and it was Hoppy Cassady with the New York Yankees. Hoppy said, 'What got George teed off?'

"I remembered we had been talking about a weight room and how we needed to improve our facility. Hoppy said to meet him at the airport and, to make a long story short, we went out and picked up equipment for a new weight room. We hadn't asked for it; Steinbrenner just sent it."

Steinbrenner was constantly sending Yankees souvenirs to Nashville fans, via the Sounds.

"Almost every day we'd get a cap or a jacket or something in the mail, with the instruction to get it to somebody Steinbrenner had promised it to."

Steinbrenner's critics claim he interferes too greatly with the on-field operation of his team. Schmittou recalls only one such instance with the Sounds.

"During our second season with the Yankees, Steinbrenner signed us some great players and we won the division," says Schmittou. "We won 97 games that year but lost to Memphis in the playoffs. We'd had two great years but still hadn't won a championship.

"I went to the playoffs and was on a plane with Steinbrenner. He asked me who the top prospects were in the Southern League. I told him, and he said he'd try to get them for us. Then he said, 'I'm not satisfied with not winning the championship. I'm going to send you a new manager, Johnny Oates.'

"I had never said a negative word about our manager, Stump Merrill. Stump had made a mistake in a big game, putting a pitcher in the outfield and forgetting about him, and had been criticized for it.

"Stump to this day thinks I got him fired, but I didn't. It was Steinbrenner's idea to make the change, not that he didn't like Stump. He did, and eventually Stump went on to manage the Yankees. Steinbrenner just saw something in Johnny Oates and wanted to get him started in managing."

Schmittou notes that Steinbrenner, during his Nashville visits, "was always cordial to the media and fans. He signed autographs and did interviews. He never did anything for the Sounds but help.

"Even after we left the Yankees and moved up to Class

AAA, when we made our major-league bid George was Nashville's best good-will ambassador. He sang the praises of the city, what a great town it is, and what a great operation the Sounds are.

"Yes, he can be impatient and controversial. He kinda gets in a hurry and people jump when he hollers. But Nashville and our ball club never had a better friend.

"If I called him today and told him there was a worthwhile cause in Nashville and we needed $10,000, I'd bet my last dime the $10,000 would be here the next day.

"That's the George Steinbrenner I know."

Another colorful, controversial big-league owner Schmittou got to know through his Sounds operations is Cincinnati Reds boss Marge Schott.

"I admire Marge," says Schmittou, "although it took awhile for us to become acquainted.

"I'd been with the Reds for three or four years and had never met Mrs. Schott. I'd always dealt with the farm director or the manager on the field. When I'd go to Cincinnati to games, I'd sit in the stands.

"In 1990 our agreement with the Reds was up. I wanted the Reds to come back to Nashville, but Mrs. Schott wanted to move the Class AAA team to Columbus, Ohio.

"Their farm director, Howie Biddell, suggested I come up to meet with her. I said, 'I don't know . . . I've heard she doesn't like me or the minor leagues. She thinks we make too much money or something.

"But I really wanted the Reds back, so finally I agreed to go meet with her. I'd heard that she likes wives and dogs. So I figured the best thing I could do was take my wife along. I told Shirley, 'We're going to go meet Marge. You all talk about kids and dogs.'

"We got to Cincinnati and went into her office and introduced ourselves. That was the first time I'd ever met Mrs. Schott. She was sitting behind her desk, surrounded by miniature dogs.

"Shirley and I sat down and they started talking. They talked for over two hours, ignoring me. They talked about our kids and our dogs. Since I had nothing else to do, I began to notice all the plaques and momentos on her walls. I saw she owned a cement company, some car companies, an asphalt paving company.

"Finally I stepped into another office to talk to Mrs. Schott's nephew. I said, 'Does she really own all those companies?'

"He said she not only owned them, she took an active role in running them. She would get up at her farm each morning and start checking on her companies. She would get to the ball park around 1 p.m. and work on baseball business, then go to the game.

"One thing I had admired about her before I met her was the fact that she always went to the Reds' games. She would sit by the dugout and sign autographs for every kid that came down.

"There aren't any other big-league owners who do that.

"I also noticed that the Reds had the lowest ticket and concession prices while paying competitive players salaries.

"Eventually I went back into Mrs. Schott's office, where she and Shirley were still talking. She said, 'I don't know if I like you, but I like your wife. Why don't you go down and get something worked out?'

"And that's how we got two more years with Cincinnati. That was my first and only face-to-face meeting with Mrs. Schott.

"She began to have problems with Jesse Jackson and some players over some racially offensive remarks she was said to have made in private. Suddenly everybody was trying to run her out of baseball.

"One day a sportswriter in Nashville, Larry Woody, called and asked me what I though about Marge Schott, who was making headlines with all the controversy. She didn't seem to have a friend or defender in the world.

"I was honest—I told the writer Marge Schott had always been fair with me and good to the Sounds, and I had a great deal of respect for her as a business person and as a baseball owner.

"I said I thought she sometimes said some things she didn't mean or shouldn't have said, and that I didn't always agree with her, but I respected her. I explained how I admired the way she signed autographs for the kids. And she was able to have the lowest prices in the major leagues, while fielding good teams.

"Well, he wrote the story and somehow a copy got sent to Mrs. Schott. One day the phone rang and my secretary, Dot Cloud, said, 'Marge Schott is on the line for you.'

"I picked up the phone and Marge was crying. I said, 'What's wrong?'

"She said, 'That article is the nicest thing anyone has ever said about me in the press. I've done some things you probably don't approve of, but I love baseball and they're trying to run me out. I'm going to fight it.

"She went on for about an hour about how much that article meant to her at that particular time. She said she didn't know what was going to happen, but she was going to fight to keep her ball team.

"I said, 'Marge, keep fighting. Don't let 'em run you out of the game.'

"I even wrote some letters for the Reds public relations office in support of Mrs. Schott, which they sent around the country. I don't know if they helped or not, but I like to think so.

"I learned that Marge Schott has her soft spots, which the public seldom sees. She is good for baseball and good for her community. She tries as hard as any owner to give her city a good team and keep the prices affordable for the working-class fan.

"Sure, she made some mistakes, like we all have. She's not very good at PR sometimes; in fact, she may be the worst at PR, if I'm not. But I admire her toughness and her determination and her devotion to her baseball team."

One of Schmittou's favorite stories involves Otis Nixon, who passed through Greer Stadium in 1980-1981 on his way to big-league stardom and riches.

"Back then we would pay the players, then we'd get reimbursed by the parent club," says Schmittou. "I got the paychecks for our players' last two weeks of the season, and most of them were for $1,100, $1,200. I noticed that Otis's check was for $1.32.

"I said, 'Otis, what's the deal here?'

"He said, 'Aw, I've had all kinds of mismanagement. I've been up to Columbus and back, run up phone bills, loaned money to a buddy . . . stuff like that.'

"He sat down and figured up what he owed and it came to about $6,000. So I said, 'Let's go meet a friend of mine, Roy McDonald, who's a banker.'

"Roy loaned Otis $6,500 and I co-signed with him. I told him to pay his interest and pay the rest back as he could. It took him awhile but he finally got it all paid back."

Nixon went on to earn millions in the majors but was plagued with drug problems.

"Otis had some personal problems," says Schmittou. "He was typical of a lot of minor-league players; baseball does a poor job educating them about how to manage their lives and their finances.

"Otis, for example, was 18 or 19 when he signed, out of a very small town in North Carolina. He was thrown out into the world. He had never been exposed to money. He didn't know how to manage his finances or his time.

"Even today we see a kid from a rural or poor background come into a big city, get thrown into the night life, getting bad habits, running with the guys. He may drink too much beer, chase too many women, whatever. That's where a lot of their problems start.

"In Class AAA it's better because most of the players have been around and a lot of them are married. Their wives keep them settled down and help manage their finances.

"But in Class AA and below, some of these players have never put down a deposit for an apartment, a telephone, lights. Then all of a sudden they get called up or down and they don't know how to handle it. I not only felt for Otis, I feel for all young players like him."

Schmittou ran into Nixon during the 1994 players' strike. He had opened his own electronics store in a mall in Atlanta, where Schmittou's daughter Debbie lived nearby.

"Shirley and I were visiting and I looked across the way and there was Otis," says Schmittou. "I went over and we began to talk. We must have talked for an hour, about his days with the Sounds, about the strike, just about baseball in general.

"He said he was doing well. He had got his life straightened out. He had remarried and had eight or nine kids.

"He seemed happy, flashing that great smile of his, and I'm happy for him."

Not all the interesting characters who came Schmittou's way were famous. One, in fact, disappeared without a trace on the eve of his scheduled wedding at Greer Stadium.

"In 1980, near the end of the season, we had a relief pitcher named Lewis," recalls Schmittou. "He was a real quiet guy. Dressed a little different. Wore his hair a little different. But then most relief pitchers are kinda different."

"A few weeks before the season ended Lewis came to my office and said, 'Coach, you ever had a marriage in the ball park, since you do all these other promotions?'

"I said, 'No, we've never had a wedding at the ball park.'

"He said, 'Well, I'd like to get married here on the last day of the season. Do you think you could get some of the merchants to pitch in?'

"I said, 'Absolutely.' So we got Castner-Knott to donate

the bride's dress, some other stores donated gifts and things, and we figured we'd get the other players on the team to hold their bats in an arch as the couple walked through.

"So everything was all set up when we came off the road for our final home stand of the season. The first day we went through the rehearsal, with the players in their tuxes and so on.

"The next day the parents of the bride, who was a student at Vanderbilt, flew in from San Francisco. They came into my office, very well-dressed and refined. Then their daughter came in with their future son-in-law, who they had never seen before.

"This strange look came over the face of the father of the bride. You could tell he didn't like what he saw. Quickly he said, 'Could you excuse us?' and they left.

"That night at the game there was no relief pitcher, no Lewis. The next night, the night of the scheduled wedding, there was no relief pitcher, no Lewis, no groom.

"I never saw him again. He never even showed up to pick up his last paycheck. I haven't seen from him or heard from him since.

"I strongly suspect that the father of the bride, after he got a look at Lewis, gave him X number of dollars not to show up for his wedding.

"And that's how our first ball-park wedding turned out to be a no-show."

Pete Rose, the Cincinnati Reds manager and all-time major-league great, was banished from baseball for his gambling activities.

Schmittou refuses to stand in judge of his off-the-field character but says he always admired the Pete Rose he knew on the ball field.

"I admired Pete for the way he played the game," says Schmittou. "He played harder than anybody. As a college coach I used to love to have a player like that on my team; he made the other players play harder.

"Rose ran to first base on a walk. He slid hard to break up a double play. He dove head-first into the bases. He played every game with all-out enthusiasm.

"When the Sounds joined the Reds, I got to meet Rose and he was always very cordial. I saw him at spring training and when the farm director introduced us, he said, 'Oh, yeah, Nashville.' He always had something nice to say.

"During our second season with the Reds, Rose would say something like, 'We need to put a better team in there.' Or, 'We need to win some games down there.'

"He had a sincerity about him. He loved the game, and he was smart.

"After he left the Reds and signed with the Phillies, I saw him going to the press conference and he was so proud—not about that fact that he was going to make a million dollars, but that he had made it for the type of player he was. He was not a home-run hitter, he was a hustler.

"He played hard and he played dirty. Not down-and-dirty, but in the dirt, the way a lot of us think the game should be played."

Schmittou says Rose's reputation for being greedy when it came to peddling his autograph at card shows was unfair.

"Yes, he did a lot of card shows for money," he says, 'but he also gave away thousands of free autographs to fans at the ball park. I remember when the Reds came here for a two-day exhibition, Rose got to the park and there must have been 500 people waiting for his autograph. He signed them all.

"During the game he sat by the dugout and signed everything that was handed to him. The next day, after the final game, he signed autographs as he walked back to the bus.

"Later on one of the talk shows, I heard some people complaining that he hadn't signed something. I'll bet during those two days here he must have signed 3,000 autographs—for free. And he did that every time he came here.

"Rose was visible, made his players visible, and made the

games seem important to our fans. He was genuinely concerned about our team. He would call every once in awhile and ask how we were doing. He was the only manager of any major-league team we were with who would do that.

"If I asked him to write a letter to a little crippled boy, he would do it."

As for the problems that drove Rose from the game:

"I never talked to him about it," says Schmittou. "He was so embarrassed and hurt. He broke the law, said he was guilty of some things, and went to prison. That part was fair.

"I think the hardest part, though, was being banned from baseball. He loves the game so much. Pete Rose had more hits than any other player who ever played major-league baseball. He has more hits than anyone and had 10 different seasons where he had 200 or more hits. No one has ever done better. he played for a World Series champion, was MVP, an All-Star. Those are the things he needs to be measured by when it comes to the Hall of Fame, not his morals.

"If you measured players by their morals, you'd have to remove a lot of the ones who are in there now. Should Pete Rose be in the Hall of Fame? Absolutely."

After Rose left prison he opened a restaurant in Florida and bought some old Atlanta Braves seats from Schmittou. He also invites Schmittou to be a guest on his nationally syndicated radio show two or three times a year.

"I regard Pete as a great player," says Schmittou, " and as a great friend."

Schmittou has known five baseball commissioners. Bowie Kuhn was his favorite, Fay Vincent his least favorite.

"Peter Ueberroth could be overbearing, but he was available," says Schmittou. "I was with the Rangers when he was commissioner. He was always abrupt, like he was in a hurry. I got the feeling the job of commissioner bored him."

Vincent succeeded Bart Giamatti, who died after serving only briefly.

"I think I'd have liked Giamatti," says Schmittou. "But when Fay Vincent took over he was the most power-grabbing person I ever knew. "He looked down his nose at everybody. Without having an investment in the game, he thought he should be able to run everything.

"My first meeting with Vincent was at the earthquake World Series in San Francisco. I was on the executive committee of the minor leagues, and Shirley and I were there for the Series and for a meeting with the commissioner.

"After the earthquake struck, we all figured the meeting would be canceled. But we were told no, the Commissioner still wanted to meet with us in his penthouse suite. Power had not been restored when we got to his hotel, where they had one elevator hooked up to a generator to get up to his suite.

"We went up and were met by two of his assistants. Vincent didn't even say hello. He didn't offer us a cup of coffee, a drink of water, anything. He immediately lit in: 'Umpires in the minor leagues don't make enough money. They're having to steal baseballs to get meal money.'

"That man didn't even know what umpires were making. Within a few weeks of that meeting, he was comparing all people to the minor leagues to popcorn salesmen. He wanted to do away with the minors.

"Vincent didn't know anything about baseball, didn't understand it. He had no baseball background. He liked to ride around in his golf cart at major-league games and be seen.

"Finally they fired him. None too soon, as far as I was concerned.

Hank Aaron, who broke Babe Ruth's home run record, was another of Schmittou's all-time favorites.

"I got to know Henry after he joined the Braves' front office," says Schmittou. "He came here several times to try to get the Sounds to sign with Atlanta, or to scout for prospects.

"He seemed kind of shy and modest, and I got the feeling he was almost embarrassed by all the attention he received from his success. I never heard him brag about what a great career he had, or about all his home runs.

"He was always cordial, and he used to embarrass me by calling me 'Mr. Schmittou.' He was a very humble guy."

Aaron has sometimes been described as a bitter man who carried a chip on his shoulder because of the shabby treatment he received from some boorish—and often racist— fans during his quest of baseball's most sacred record. He kept much of the hate mail he received during that period.

"I don't claim to know what he went through," says Schmittou, "but from what I've read and heard, some of it was pretty bad.

"But I don't know that it was only a black-white thing. There's a certain segment of society that likes to run down and cheapen other people's accomplishments. I think that may have been the case with Henry. But I never saw any bitterness at all in Aaron. He never mentioned it or revealed it in any of his actions or manners.

"He was always gracious, respectful of people, the perfect gentleman. I've ridden on buses with him at the World Series and never once heard him say a critical word about anyone.

"One funny story: We used to have a guy working for us named Rags Drennon who we called our equipment technician. One day Aaron was visiting Greer Stadium and old Rags walked up and slapped him on the back and said, 'How ya doin' Willie?' He thought Aaron was Willie Mays.

"Aaron never let on. He just smiled and said, 'I'm doing fine.' It was like he didn't want to embarrass Rags. That kinda typified the kind of person he was."

Schmittou claims Aaron hit one home run for which he was never credited.

"I was in Atlanta Stadium at the time and they had an outfield fence that was glass. Aaron hit a line drive to right center that was so hard it went over the glass, bounced off the wall behind it, and bounced back onto the field. The umpire ruled it a double, but I knew that ball had gone out, and so did Aaron.

"But he pulled up at second and never argued."

When Aaron hit the home run that broke Ruth's record, Schmittou recalls "sitting in my living room, watching with the rest of the world. I was so happy for him.

"He was a great, great player and he deserved every honor he received. I respected him before I met him, and after I got to know him I respected him even more.

"Nobody has more class and dignity than Henry Aaron."

Schmittou became acquainted with another "living legend" of a vastly different nature: Morganna, baseball's famous Kissing Bandit.

She was an exotic dancer who became nationally famous for darting onto the field during games and planting a smooch on a player.

"When I was with the Rangers she was performing at a strip joint in Fort Worth and there were rumors that she was planning to run onto our field and kiss Buddy Bell," recalls Schmittou.

"One day I got a phone call. It was Morganna, who remembered me from Vanderbilt. She wanted to know if I would have her arrested if she ran onto our field. I said, 'Yes, I will—just like I'd have anyone else arrested.'

"She thanked me and hung up. We never saw anything of her."

When Morganna was dancing in Nashville's famed Printer's Alley, she called Schmittou to request Vanderbilt football tickets, but she never turned up at Greer Stadium.

"Every year she sends baseball general managers a cartoon Christmas card that, well, kinda reveals her assets," chuckles Schmittou. "I think I've still got one of those cards hidden somewhere around here."

Yogi Berra is famous for such illogical come-again one liners as, "It ain't over till it's over," and "Nobody comes here anymore; it's too crowded."

Schmittou discovered a sharp mind hiding behind the sharp wit.

"Yogi is one of the smartest men I've ever met in baseball," he says. "During the 1981 strike the Yankees sent their coaches to work with their farm clubs, and Yogi was assigned to Nashville.

"He'd sit in the press box, quiet, watching the game. He was like Jim Turner—you could carry on a conversation with him and he'd talk, but his eyes never left the field.

"He never took a note, and after three home stands he must have watched about 20 games. At the end of the last stand, he went down to coaches' office and began to quote inning-by-inning things he had observed. He had stored everything in his head and could recall every detail from memory. I don't know anybody else who could do that.

"He made great business deals and investments, he knew baseball, and he was smart. But one time I just had to ask him: 'Yogi, did you really say all those things that have been attributed to you over the years?'

"He looked me right in the eye and said, 'Probably 75 percent of them are true and the other half aren't.'"

One of baseball's most famous minor-leaguers was a player whose first impression on Schmittou was, "He was not as good as any of the 15-year-olds I used to coach on my youth teams."

His name was Michael Jordan, who almost became a Sound.

"When I heard that Jordan had 'retired' from the NBA and was going to play professional baseball, I thought is was just a publicity stunt—and I still do," says Schmittou.

Jordan spent his first season with the Class AA Birmingham Barons, and Schmittou observed him during spring training.

"A coach had to stand behind the fence in right field and

tell him what to do," says Schmittou. "He didn't know how to play a routine fly ball, he couldn't hit Class A pitching, he had no feel for the game. I thought he was just a terrible player who had no business in professional baseball on any level."

Nashville at the time had a Class AA team as well as the Class AAA Sounds, and the Barons made several visits to Greer Stadium.

"The first time they came in, Jordan was batting about .110," says Schmittou. "He was not only terrible at the plate, but in one game one of our guys hit a deep fly to right and Jordan didn't know which way to play the ball. He started the wrong way, kinda stumbled around, lunged at the ball at the last second, and somehow it landed in his glove.

"We had a packed house, and the fans gave him a standing ovation. I turned to a guy standing beside me and said, 'That's the first time I've ever seen anybody get a standing ovation for misplaying a routine fly ball.'"

Jordan gradually began to win Schmittou's admiration with his dedicated work ethic.

"The next day I saw him walk into the stadium at 11:30 for a 2:00 game," recalls Schmittou. "He went to right field and a coach began to bat him fly balls. He knew how badly he had misplayed the ball the previous night.

"The next time he came to town, he was really in a slump. He looked awful the first night. The next day he came to the stadium about 2:30 and that's when I began to gain respect for him. He started taking batting practice. An hour and a half later, he was still taking batting practice.

"It became a routine with him. Jordan would come in early and take 200 or 300 extra swings with the bat. As a former coach, I had to admire that. He worked awfully hard to try to make himself a better player.

"He came to Nashville a total of five times that season and I'll have to say this: The last time I could see marked improvement. He had improved his defense, he was a good base runner, and he had developed enough batting skills that at least the pitcher had to actually pitch to him, rather than just blow a ball past him.

"His work ethic was tremendous, and he inspired excellent work habits in the other players. They saw this guy who was supposed to be the greatest athlete in the world, putting in all that extra work, so they worked harder, too.

"I still don't think he was a good player, by professional standards, but he never hung his head and quit."

Despite Jordan's struggles in Class AA, the White Sox announced plans to promote him to their Class AAA club in Nashville in the spring of 1994.

Schmittou's phone immediately began to ring.

"I was getting calls from the local media, from the West Coast, even a call from Alaska," he says. "I tried to tell everybody that it didn't mean anything until he actually reported. We were bending over backwards to explain to people that there was no assurance Jordan would be with the club, but the ticket orders kept pouring in."

Schmittou began to plan some promotions around the possible Michaelmania. He taped some TV spots, one of which showed him wearing a shaved-head wig, a la His Airness.

"He would have sold a lot of tickets," says Schmittou, "but down deep I suspected he was not going to play baseball. In January his agent told me to arrange housing and various things for him, but every time I'd ask about specifics, it would be, 'Well, we're not quite ready for that.' I could tell they were delaying.

"Sure enough, just a couple of days after Jordan announced he was returning to the NBA, McDonald's already had some commercials done. I personally suspect the whole thing was orchestrated—very magnificently—to increase his marketability when he went back to the Chicago Bulls."

Schmittou harbors no ill will toward Jordan or his last-minute snub of the Sounds.

"He was good for the game from the standpoint that he attracted a lot of attention," says Schmittou.

"Could he have ever made it to the big leagues? Maybe, someday, if he had continued to work the way I saw him work. There's a chance he might have gone there. But now we'll never know."

Chapter XII
The Name of the Game
Is Putting Fannies
in the Seats

B aseball may be the love of Larry Schmittou's life, but it's also a serious business.

"I'm a lucky man, because I get to make a living in a game that I've always been extremely fond of," he says.

"I get asked quite often which I liked best—being a coach or an employer. Well, I'd rather own 1 percent of something and work in it than own no percent and work for the biggest company in the world. I like to be in charge and control my own destiny. I don't like to invest in things I have no say in.

"After all the years of working for somebody else—at the Ford Glass plant, in the Metro school system, and at Vanderbilt—it was quite a change to start my own business with the Sounds. Remember, I had very little experience in the business world. Actually, I had only one experience and that was building houses, and I had no previous knowledge of that industry. It was an expensive venture.

"I was extremely fortunate to be surrounded by older, experienced friends who gave me advice whenever I needed it. And I needed it a lot back in those days.

"Most people say entrepreneurs usually fail in their first endeavor. In fact, eight out of 10 businesses probably don't make it past 10 years.

"Now, when people ask me what they should do when starting their own business, I advise them about what I did when starting my baseball business. Take about 60 to 90 days to thoroughly research whether this is right for you, especially if you already have a good job.

"Prepare yourself about how you are going to put the business together. Do some soul-searching and some research. I suggest reading some good books on the subject and would recommend *In Search of Excellence* by Tom Peters and Robert Waterman Jr., and especially concentrate on chapters 1, 6, 8, 9, 10, and 11, which really give some parameters on what it takes to have a successful business.

"After you complete that book, I would recommend Mark McCormack's book *What They Still Don't Teach You at Harvard Business School*. I would pay particular attention to the main topics, starting with the introduction, 'The Ten Commandments of Street Smarts.' Other key parts of the book deal with negotiating and getting organized.

"Then I'd say go on to two other good, easy-reading books by Harvey MacKay, *Swim With the Sharks Without Being Eaten Alive* and *Beware of the Naked Man Who Offers You His Shirt*.

"They provide a common-sense guide to how to run a successful business, how to treat people, and how to determine if running a business is really your cup of tea.

"If after reading these books you still feel you have the intestinal fortitude to tackle a business, and that's what you want to do, you should do extensive research into the area you are interested in. If it's a restaurant, for example, try to observe all types of restaurants—the good, the bad, and the in-between—to determine what's good and bad.

"In my case, I visited as many baseball parks as I could and observed their operations. I knew a little about baseball, but I didn't know how to run a team from the standpoint of revenue and expenses. So I tried to study all the ones I could, especially the successful ones, to where I could copy their best ideas.

"As I mentioned earlier, George Sisler and Dick Fitzpatrick at Columbus were the most help to me, but all the clubs I visited were beneficial—even the bad ones. They taught me the things you don't want to do when you start your own business.

"After that, you need three or four very key people and I was fortunate to come up with the right ones in my venture into business: a very good lawyer, good bankers that believed in me, and a good CPA.

"In my case, I hooked up with attorney John Reynolds. He was a friend who knew I didn't have much money, so he structured a limited partnership with me being the general partner, whereby I didn't have to own 50 percent to have control. If you are fortunate enough to own 100 percent, that's ideal; but if you're not able to do that, I'd suggest looking into a limited partnership, a limited liability corporation, or if you go to a corporation, have such a good management contract that you protect your interest, especially if you're in business with people who have more money than you.

"Second, you need a very good accountant. Again, I was fortunate to be recommended to Kraft Brothers, a local accounting firm. Lee Kraft had been my accountant for years and he helped me formulate a business plan and research my numbers. A friend of Jerry Reed's, Colleen Chapple of Chapple Business Service, enabled me to set up a business practice, then sent me to a banker to show them a plan I had to attract other investors.

"I could sit down with the investors and show them this is how we will be organized, this is what each percent will cost, this is how much you should expect to receive as a return on your money, and when you should get that return.

"I made many, many mistakes along the way. I would advise anybody when they start doing their planning and budgets, when you list your projected revenues and your expenses, when you get through, go back and reduce your revenue by 10 percent and increase your expenses by 10 percent. Then you'll be pretty accurate, especially in your early, formative years.

"Then, when you have done all this, you are ready to recruit investors.

"When I started the Sounds in 1977 I made one very big mistake. I decided to raise $300,000, and I, being the general partner, would buy 10 percent, or two units of our 20 units issued, for a total of $30,000. My bankers agreed to loan me the money.

"Then I went out to find the other people to invest $15,000 for each 5 percent. That was really the only criteria: who had $15,000. I didn't ask what their philosophies were. I painted too rosy a picture about when they would get their money back. I never dreamed—or, rather, had any nightmare—that the stadium would cost so much and that we would have to keep investing longer than I had projected to get the investment back.

"I also did not look for good chemistry. I should have known that, because a partnership is very much like coaching a football or baseball team. You have to have a chemistry, and everyone must know their roles. Everyone must know who the captain is and recognize who the coach is. This was a very bad mistake on my part, even though I recruited people who liked baseball.

"Some thought they were just doing it as a community endeavor, some wanted their money back the next day, and others were in it for the long haul.

"I would strongly advise anybody doing it now to take their time to recruit partners with the same general philosophy.

"It took me about five years to correct this mistake, and at a fair negotiated price we bought out about five of our original investors. They were good people; they just had different philosophies. "I know now that if I'd been a little more selective and had more knowledge, this was a situation that probably would not have occurred.

"A funny story about my first owners' meeting in 1978: We had drawn very well that year, but we were still trying to build the stadium, so we were always short on money. We had a meeting and went over everything, and Walter Nipper, owner of Nashville Sporting Goods and now the second-largest shareholder of the Sounds, stood up at the meeting after I explained exactly where we were, and made this statement: 'Larry, you might be the worst businessman in Nashville.'

"I simply looked at Walter and said, 'You're probably right.' But I made up my mind he wouldn't be able to say that the next year.

"I learned an awfully lot from Walter Nipper. He's a smart businessman who has built a fortune by starting sporting goods stores and branching out into real estate and investing in people.

"Then there was the Reese Smith family, which has a large home building business. Reese Smith Jr., who passed away a few years ago, was very influential. He was different from Walter in some ways and like him in others. Reese was skilled with politicians, which I never was, but I learned a lot of other things from Reese and his sons, Reese III, Steve, and Mark.

"Jerry Reed, a great friend and a great supporter, is someone who teaches people how to relax by laughing at themselves.

"Another entertainer-investor, Richard Sterban of the Oak Ridge Boys, is excellent with public relations.

"Later, other people came aboard—Bill Wilson, Lew Conner, Roscoe Buttrey, and the late Bronson Ingram—and I learned a great deal from all of them.

"After your investors, the next most important people are the ones you surround yourself with on a day-to-day basis: your employees.

"You must be willing to accept the responsibility of having an extended family. When you hire employees, you are greatly affecting their lives, and you often spend more time with them than you do with your own family.

"You must put the right people in the right positions, just as you do with a ball team. Some positions are obviously more important than others. You need some entry-level people, people you can train, people you can afford. Start with fewer people than you think you will need. It's always easier to add people later than it is to lay people off.

"We've been fortunate with the Sounds; we've never had to lay anybody off. That comes from planning and letting the business grow at its own pace.

"We started small, and we didn't spend money we didn't have. I hired some very good people, starting with Farrell Owens. He was a schoolteacher who taught by day and worked for us during the night at first. He was great in public relations, meeting people, and working in sales during a very critical period of our development.

"My second hire was Mrs. Jeanne Carney, as a secretary. Her family loved sports, she enjoyed what she was doing, and I'm proud to say that 18 years later she is still with us.

"We hired a young lady, Geri Schranz, who was great with the public. She worked in accounts receivable as well as media relations. She was a very attractive lady and the media wanted to run our stories just to make sure they pleased her.

"We started our business with two full-time employees making about minimum wage, one part-time employee, Farrell, and, actually, a second part-time employee—me. I kept my day job, coaching at Vanderbilt, for the first year.

"Everyone else was hired on a day-to-day basis, such as concession workers, grounds crew, ushers, ticket-takers, and we just kind of grew as our business went along.

"That first year we had approximately 70-100 game-day employees. We grossed about $1 million.

"Since that time we have grown to what would be considered an average Class AAA franchise. We have 11 full-time employees and during the season we add between 200 and 250 part-time workers. Today we are about a $4 million-a-year company."

Most minor-league clubs' front offices break down as follows: a general manager who may also be the CEO; an assistant GM who may also have a title of director of marketing; and the ticket manager and staff.

"In our franchise my son Ronnie, who started in an entry-level job, has worked his way up to director of marketing," says Schmittou.

"Our ticket manager is Dot Cloud, who I consider to be the best in baseball because of her great PR skills. Most clubs also have a group sales director; in our case this position is handled by D. Smith.

"Our office manager is Sharon Carson, who also serves as a personal secretary and handles all accounts receivable.

"The team's business manager keeps up with the money, and one thing you can never afford to do is run short of cash. In our case we double that job up with our marketing manager, Ronnie.

"You need a director of media relations to work with the press, keep up with stats, and put out releases. Ours is Robbie Bohren, who came from Vanderbilt University and the Texas Rangers.

"You usually need two people in stadium operations. For the Sounds they are Brad Dennis, who is assisted by Brad Myers. They oversee all stadium operations from ticket takers and ushers to parking and maintenance. They also double as sales people in the off-season.

"Our director of concessions is Walt Mehlenbacher, who handles all food and beverage concessions as well as our stadium club and suites.

"My son Mike is director of merchandising and promotions. He is in charge of all our mail orders and souvenir sales, and he handles such special promotions as the Famous Chicken. Mike, like everybody else, is also in sales.

"The groundskeeper is very important, and we have one of the best in Dave Nasypany.

"We're also assisted by two 18-year employees, Jeanne Carney and Doris Taylor, who work full time in tickets.

"As you notice, all our people have something in common: they sell. They sell baseball. They sell tickets. They sell advertising. They sell concessions. They sell good will. We're in the selling business all year long, 365 days a year.

"That's the allure of minor-league baseball. You get to sell a product you believe in, to people who want to buy."

"The support people may be the most important ones of all because they come in such close contact with the fans. It's important to have good, courteous concession workers, ushers, and so on. These are the people who make the greatest impression on the fans, and go a long way in determining whether a franchise is successful or not."

Schmittou made baseball not just an enjoyable business but a successful one as well.

"Over the years we have owned nine different baseball teams, one hockey team, one basketball team and two concession companies. We have invested less than $1,000,000 of our own money. During that time we have sold eight of the baseball teams for a little over $12 million, and we still have the most valuable one, our Nashville Sounds, which is valued at over $10 million.

"Investing in baseball is a lot like anything else. You have to learn to negotiate, to see how badly someone wants to sell one of these teams, whether you can buy at a low a price and arrange favorable financing.

"If you're smart, careful, and willing to work hard, you can do OK with a minor-league franchise. I have always shied away from taking over the super-successful franchises for two reasons: they cost too much money and, as I've stated before, it's awfully hard to follow a superstar and be successful.

"In all the clubs we have bought we have been able to go in with entirely new management, which is important for the reasons I've already stated. You can pick and choose your own people and put them in positions they best fit.

"You also need good timing to buy a business. We were fortunate to buy our franchises at a time when most people were selling their teams for what they owed on them. They questioned whether we could make a profit on them. We quickly started putting some marketing ideas together that worked in the 1970's and 1980's and more good people kept buying minor-league clubs and applying good business principles.

"We learned from each other, attending seminars and exchanging ideas. Anyone who is getting into baseball should be required to attend Jim Paul's seminar in El Paso each year. I've gone many years, either as a speaker or spectator. I would always come away with five or six ideas. I'd put them into effect, and usually four or five would work out. That's how you keep coming up with new promotions and ideas.

"When we first started buying clubs in 1977 we paid $7,500 for a Southern League franchise. That's about all any were worth at that time. Now any class AA club, which is what we were in 1977, is going for $4 million to $6 million just for the right to do business.

"A good Class AAA franchise will go for anywhere from $7 million to $10 million and up. A Class A franchise usually sells in the range of $2 million to $5 million. Keep in mind that we once paid $16,000 and change for a team in Salem because that's what they owed their popcorn company.

"I can honestly say we never bought a club with the intention of turning around and selling it in two or three years. All the clubs we sold were sold because people came to us and made us an offer of more than seven years' projected earnings. We felt like it was a sound business decision because we weren't living in those cities. But we sold only to people who were carefully screened to make sure they would be good owners., leaving the franchise in that community, and do as good or better job running it as if we were there.

"Sometimes owners forget the responsibility we have; we are stewards of that franchise. Franchises should be owned by the fans.

"During our 18 years of ownership, we have also looked at buying parts of major-leagues clubs. In 1984 we made an offer to buy the Pittsburgh Pirates from the Galbreath family. At that time the franchises were going for about $20 million. Fortunately for the city of Pittsburgh, the Galbreaths sold to a group of businessmen who kept the team there for 10 years, and as we're speaking they're going through new ownership.

"We also looked at buying an American League club in the 1990's. By that time the prices had escalated to $70 million to $80 million. We thought we had an investor lined up but he decided to wait until another major-league club opened up in his hometown, which it later did, and he purchased it."

"To be honest, you sometimes wonder why anyone wants to own a major-league club because of the expense. The average major-league club in today's market has an expense of $25 million to $28 million in salaries for a 25-man active roster. They also spend about $9 million on their player development systems—six or seven minor-league teams, along with scouts, signing bonuses and related expenses.

"So now we're around $35 million to $40 million in costs, and we haven't bought a bat or ball yet. The administrative costs run $2 million to $3 million, covering front office, coaches, general manager, trainer, assistants, and so on.

"You have to fly teams around and most major-leaguers travel by charter. Restrictions are very strong because of the players' union. If you don't fly charter, you have to buy all first-class tickets or three coach tickets for every two players. All this travel, plus hotel expenses, will exceed another $1 million or so.

"Also there are costs for marketing, lease, insurance, workman's compensation—another $3 million to $5 million.

"Then you're finally ready to buy equipment and get ready for spring training. That's about $2 million more.

"So you can see that the average major-league club is going to spend a minimum of $40 to $50 million. That's what you have to make each year just to break even.

"Under the 1996 TV contract, each major-league club will receive between $9 million and $10 million and another $2 million from the sale of major-league licensed products.

"Now we're up to about $12 million in revenue in what is called the 'central fund,' which is money that goes to the commissioner's office and is divided among the 28 major-league teams.

"In baseball, major and minor leagues, we try to figure spending per fan. The revenue comes primarily from a very small area of services. Tickets average about $12 per person in the majors. Food and beverage contracts are usually sold to a large concession company for some up-front money plus a percentage of the gross, usually between 35 and 40 percent. The average major-league club does in the area of $5.50 per person through concessions, about $2.20 of which goes to the owner.

"So now we're up to $14.20 per fan. Most clubs also run their own novelties stands, and the average fan spends about $1 or $1.50. That puts it at $15-$16 per fan.

"A lot of clubs have their own parking, which costs about $4 per car, and each car carries an average of three fans.

"Other revenue comes from club restaurants, which seat only 300 or 400 persons, so for a total crowd the average is only around $.75 a fan.

"Add it all together and each person in the park spends about $18. If you draw two million fans you'll do about $36 million in revenue. Now you're up to about $47 million counting your share of league TV money.

"All that's left is local radio and TV—which in a mid-sized city comes to $4 million or $5 million net. Ball park advertising at most brings in $1 million to $1.5 million. Program sales and advertising runs $500,000 to $600,000.

"Most clubs have luxury suites and price differs from club to club. But the average is probably about 30 suites at $30,000 each per year.

"Total all the revenue up and it comes to $55 million to $65 million, based on two million attendance per season. That's why the name of the game in the majors and minors is putting fannies in the seats.

"Even when things go right, the average major-league team makes several million less than their highest-paid player."

(Outlined on the following two pages are the financial operations of both an average major league team and an average AA team.)

"Owning a minor-league team is a lot of different from owning a major-league team. We don't control our players in the minors, for example.

"In the 1950's and early 1960's almost all minor-league teams were about to go out of business. So the majors started what they called a 'player development contract,' which spelled out how much of the minor-league's expenses they would be willing to share.

"If it were not for the fact that the major leagues heavily subsidize the minors, no minor-league club could make a profit, and we wouldn't have minor-league baseball as we know it.

"The majors spend about 20 percent of their budget on recruiting and developing players and as a public relations tool to build interest in more than 150 minor-league communities in the U.S. and Canada.

"Under the contract between major and minor leagues, the majors own all the players, coaches and managers. They pay the meal money and even supply the equipment and training supplies. (A Class AAA player on the road gets $18-a-day meal money; a major-leaguer gets $68.)

"It requires the average minor-leaguer about five years to work his way into the majors and only a small percentage ever make it. Today I classify minor-league players in three categories: rookie and Class A guys are happy and thrilled just to be playing; Class AA players still have that gleam in their eye and know they have a true chance of moving on up; in Class AAA you have one group coming up, one group being sent down,

AVERAGE AAA BUDGET

REVENUE

Ticket Sales	(250,000 @ $4)	$1,000,000
Concession Sales	(250,000 @ $4)	1,000,000
Advertising		700,000
Parking		100,000
Souvenirs		125,000
Suites		150,000
Stadium Club		100,000
Miscellaneous		25,000
	TOTAL	$3,200,000

EXPENSES

Administrative		$900,000
Park		300,000
Team		200,000
Parking		50,000
Game		250,000
Concession		650,000
Souvenirs		80,000
Advertising		125,000
Stadium Club		90,000
Rent		300,000
	TOTAL	$2,945,000

TOTAL REVENUE	$3,200,000
TOTAL EXPENSES	$2,945,000
DIFFERENCE IN REVENUE & EXPENSES	$ 255,000

(Note: The Nashville Sounds have fared better than the average franchise, even though the team is the only one in professional baseball that built its own stadium.)

AVERAGE MAJOR LEAGUE BUDGET
(Based on 2 million fans attendance)

REVENUE*

Ticket Sales**		$24,000,000
National TV		9,500,000
Local TV and Radio		5,000,000
Concession Net Revenue (2,000,000 @ $2.25)		4,500,000
Promotions/Program Advertising		1,500,000
Signage Net		1,000,000
Parking Net		2,500,000
Souvenirs		2,000,000
Suites		1,500,000
Stadium Club Net		1,500,000
Miscellaneous		300,000
	TOTAL	$53,300,000

EXPENSES

Major League Salaries (including benefits)		$29,000,000
Player Development/Scouting		9,000,000
Team Administration		2,500,000
Team Travel		1,000,000
Spring Training Net		500,000
Marketing/Finance/Other Administrative Costs		4,000,000
Team Equipment and Clubhouse		1,000,000
Rent		3,000,000
Central Fund		2,500,000
Miscellaneous		500,000
	TOTAL	$53,000,000

TOTAL REVENUE	$53,300,000
TOTAL EXPENSES	53,000,000
DIFFERENCE IN REVENUE & EXPENSES	$300,000

* Very few major league teams enjoy all these revenue sources.
** Each fan less than 2 million means a decrease in revenue of about $18 per person.

and some who see their career coming to an end. A lot of people in our game call this level the whiners."

"As far as I'm concerned, Class AAA is the toughest for a manager because he has to have great baseball knowledge as well as being a psychologist to work with all these different types of personalities.

"We've had some great managers in Nashville. Our current manager, Rick Renick, is a big-league manager who happens to be in Class AAA right now. He's one of the best I've ever seen in any sport, working with people.

"In the minors, if a player is struggling the general manager can't just pick up the phone and say 'Get rid of this guy,' as the fans may expect him to. We have to keep in mind the main purpose in the minors is to develop and furnish players for the majors.

"The cold fact is, only one of 20 minor-leaguers signed ever makes it to the big leagues. Of the ones who get to AAA, maybe 60 percent to 70 percent go on up.

"Our job as a minor-league franchise is to provide a good stadium, well-groomed playing field, and other facilities for our players and fans. Also, we promote and market the game.

"Financially we are responsible for all transportation, which in Class AAA is primarily by air. We also pick up the hotel bills on the road for all 30 traveling members and give a portion of our ticket proceeds to the major-league team to help pay for equipment, salaries, and so on.

"I'm often asked how much a minor-league player makes. An average AAA salary is around $20,000 per year. Many of these players go down and play in winter leagues and pick up another $5,000 to $6,000. An average AA player is lucky to make between $6,000 and $8,000 for their five months of play.

"Keep in mind, the average major-league salary in 1995 was just under $1.1 million. It's very evident why minor-leaguers are so determined to realize their dream of getting to the big leagues. I just wish they could live their dream and not let money become such an issue once they get there."

Where does winning fit into the minor-league equation?

"It's very much an important part of their development," says Schmittou. "The great Bear Bryant used to say if winning wasn't important, why keep score? Bryant said he only recruited winners.

"Most minor-league players are signed out of winning programs, either in high school or college. You don't want to mentally affect them by saying winning is not important. However, the fact is, winning is only one part of their development on the minor-league level. It's not the primary reason the minors exist. Our mission is to develop players for the majors as quickly as possible."

One season the Sounds found themselves locked in a tight pennant race when the parent club, the Cincinnati Reds, called up some key players to assist in the Reds' own pennant chase. Schmittou, famous for his fierce winning desire, did not complain.

"It's just a fact of life in the minors," he explained. "The only time getting players called up like that makes me ill is when they are not used.

"I never get upset if I'm with a good organization, because I know they'll have good players at the next level and they'll simply move up a player to replace the one they called up.

"We always market our players as potential all-stars. That turned out to be the case for Don Mattingly and Willie McGee, two of the more than 100 Sounds who have made it the big leagues."

Schmittou takes obvious pride in seeing his Sounds advance their careers.

"If you don't genuinely love the game then you shouldn't be in it," he says. "Personally I'd like to see anyone who buys a club take at least a 90-day course in the sport, its history, and how it's supposed to be run. They should appreciate their responsibility and be aware of some of the game's problems so they can better deal with them and not become part of the problem.

"Some players, for example, have taken advantage of some owners by getting lucrative contracts, when the owner didn't understand that when one salary got out of line, then 24 other knocks will be coming at his door pretty quickly.

All four big-league sports—baseball, football, hockey, and basketball—are in serious financial trouble, and for the same reason: the owners paid a tremendously high price for the franchise, they are not making a reasonable return on their investment, and the players are simply making too much money for the amount of revenue being generated.

"That's why there is such a lack of stability right now. Owners are seeking more revenue in order to make a profit, so they're more than ready to move and go rape another city.

"That's happening in our city of Nashville as this book is being written. Cities are offering millions of dollars to get teams to relocate. You have to wonder what cities the teams will look to next if things don't go well.

"I don't know what the fans' breaking point will be. But I know that personally I am more and more turned off by some of the things going on, such as franchise moves, free agency, player moves, and steeper prices.

"Hopefully, all of us in professional sports can learn something from our college teams: Let's not run off and leave our fans."

SPEAKING OF SCHMITTOU...

Tennessee Governor Don Sundquist: "When I served in Congress, I was founder of the Congressional Minor League Baseball Caucus and got to know Larry Schmittou during that time. He has been a tireless promoter of baseball in Tennessee and the driving force behind the Nashville Sounds, long one of the most successful minor-league franchises. Larry is well respected within baseball circles, both for his business skills and for his obvious love of the game."

***

Bobby Bragan, former major-league manager, current executive with the Texas Rangers: "Larry Schmittou makes his mark wherever he travels. Larry and his wife and family were of tremendous help in their contribution to the Texas Rangers. He is a super salesman. He goes about doing things without fanfare. He is steady as a rock and you can stake your life on what he tells you. He is my kind of man."

***

Walter Nipper, Nashville sporting goods executive and original Sounds investor: "Nobody has done more for sports in Nashville, and received less credit, than Larry Schmittou."

***

Lee Kraft, of Kraft Brothers CPA: "It had to be someone like Larry Schmittou who inspired the George Bernard Shaw saying that some people see things as they are and ask 'Why?' while others dream of things that never were and ask 'Why not?' Larry doesn't know the meaning of the word can't. Plus, you can't outwork him—that's a winning combination."

***

Johnny Oates, former Sounds manager and current manager of the Texas Rangers: "Larry Schmittou has the properties of a man of steel and man of velvet. If there is a tough business decision to be made or a responsibility to be acted on, Larry can be a man of steel. If there is a need for listening or compassionate advice, Larry can be a man of velvet."

***

Jeanne Carney, the Sounds first paid employee: "I have been working for Larry Schmittou for 18 years now, and I can honestly say he is one of the most honest bosses I have ever had. He treats everyone the same and will not ask you to do anything he himself would not do. He works with us instead of bossing us."

***

Jim Anglea, former Sounds groundskeeper, now head grounds director with the Texas Rangers: "Larry Schmittou was always there for anyone who ever worked or played for him. In my book, he's The Man.

***

Fred Russell, senior sports editor emeritus of *The Nashville Banner*: "Larry Schmittou is one of the truest baseball men I've ever known. He is one of the most knowledgeable, competent, and in-the-trenches club operators in the business, minor or major league."

***

John Bibb, retired sports editor of the *Tennessean*: "Some people call Larry Schmittou stubborn. I'd say the word should be consistent. He's determined to do things his way, and it's hard to argue with the results. He's probably closer to the man on the street than anybody in Nashville sports history, at any level. He proved Vanderbilt could win the Southeastern Conference in baseball and proved professional baseball can succeed in Nashville when a lot of us kept telling him he couldn't."

***

Dot Cloud, Sounds ticket manager: "1996 will be my 12th season to work for and with Larry Schmittou. I have had the opportunity to see a side of Larry that few people have ever seen. I have mailed his personal checks for such things as the funeral expenses for a Sounds bat boy; a 6-year-old fan in the hospital for cancer treatment; a woman whose home burned and her child would have had no Christmas; scholarships for many young men and women who could not go to college without help. He is both tough and tender. My job has been fun, with a great boss, every single day for 12 years."

***

Chuck Ross, Sounds number-one fan: "Larry has always been good to me. He's my best buddy."

***

Jim Fyke, director of Metro Parks: "Larry Schmittou and I became friends in 1964, and I think the world of him. Sometimes Larry is his own worst enemy, though, because he's so determined to accomplish what he desires that he thinks everybody else should be just as single-minded. Today's world is about compromise, and Larry Schmittou is willing to do very little of it."

***

Fred Pancoast, former Vanderbilt football coach and prominent insurance executive: "I worked with Larry Schmittou under unusual circumstances: He was my football recruiter at the same time he single-handedly energized Vanderbilt's baseball program. He has done more for baseball than anybody I know. He's an aggressive, competitive businessman, but underneath it he's a very good man."

***

Former Nashville mayor Richard Fulton: "Larry Schmittou speaks his mind and seldom, if ever, changes his opinion on an issue related to sports. He has been good for baseball and good for Nashville. Baseball in Middle Tennessee was given a transfusion and a new life when Larry Schmittou and his partners invested their time and money in the Sounds."

***

Ron Bargatze, former basketball coach and current Vanderbilt color commentator: "Larry Schmittou is as driven and savvy a person as I know. Whether it's on the field or in the office, he wins the old-fashioned way: a sound game plan and hard work. He is Nashville's premier professional sports pioneer."

***

Chuck Morgan, former Sounds announcer, now director of in-park entertainment for the Texas Rangers: "With three inches of snow on the ground in January 1978, I went to Greer Stadium to apply for the position of public address announcer. Larry gave me the job for $15 a game. I didn't care about the money; I just wanted to be a part of professional baseball in Nashville. Before that, I was pretty much kept in the bowels of WSM radio and TV. Suddenly, because of my work with the Sounds, WSM wanted me doing television and radio sports and eventually the Grand Ole Opry and a nationwide satellite radio show. I followed Larry to Texas where I got to call Nolan Ryan's 5,000th strikeout, and it can now be heard when you go to Cooperstown to visit the Baseball Hall of Fame. It all started with Larry saying, back in those first days with the Sounds, 'Chuck, let's do something to get this crowd going!' Thanks, Larry, for giving Chuck Morgan a chance."

***

Alexander Heard, former Chancellor, Vanderbilt University (1963 to 1982): "Coach Schmittou made important contributions to the Vanderbilt baseball program. We were distressed to see him go."

***

Dave Fendrick, Texas Rangers Corporate Marketing Director: "I feel Larry Schmittou is one of three people in minorleague baseball that changed the entire landscape. In the mid-

1970's Larry was one who saw the potential of minor-league ball and turned the entire thing into a business venture so the minor leagues could make some money. He is the first to arrive at the park and the last to leave. Larry is a true mentor of mine."

***

Steve Sloan, former Vanderbilt football coach and current athletics director at the University of South Florida: "Larry Schmittou is one of the most interesting and memorable people I have ever met. He has a great sense of humor and an uncommon understanding of people. His work ethic is extraordinary, as well as his creativity. I was most impressed with his love and loyalty to his family."

***

Jim Ballweg, Houston Astros advertising and broadcasting sales and former Sounds PR director: "Larry Schmittou is truly Mr. Baseball in Middle Tennessee. Larry not only knows the in and outs of the game on both the field and as an owner, he genuinely cares about the game. I am very grateful that he gave me the opportunity to live and learn America's greatest sport."

***

Rod Dedeaux, retired USC baseball coach who in 45 years won five straight national championships (1970–1974) and a total of 10: "I had great admiration for Larry Schmittou as a college coach. He taught me a great lesson about coaching, because I have never been able to beat him. To get him out of coaching I contributed to get him a ball club so I wouldn't have to coach against him again. His success is no surprise to me, as he had contributed greatly to the game."

***

Paul Baugh, Greer Stadium Club chef: "Larry Schmittou is a man of great integrity who I have known for 15 years, 14 of them working for him. The city of Nashville should be grateful to have Mr.Schmittou. He treats fans with respect, and he treats me like one of his sons."

***

Jimmy Bragan, former president, Southern League: "I count Larry Schmittou as one of pro baseball's better operators. He is a big-leaguer, and I count him among one of my best, most respected friends."

***

Jerry Hampton, senior vice president, First American National Bank: "Growing up in Davidson County and playing sports all my life, I had heard about and read about Larry Schmittou. My association with him began a few years back when I represented my bank in a financial transaction with the Sounds. I have found him to be a man of great integrity, a great storyteller, and a pleasure to know. He often gets a bad rap for being outspoken, but saying what you believe and believing what you say isn't such a bad trait."

***

Tom Powell, senior vice-president, Suntrust Bank, and '73 Vanderbilt co-captain: "Whether on a bus ride gin-rummy game with sportswriter Jimmy Davy or going nose-to-nose with Eddie Stanky, Larry Schmittou was a competitor. From youth sandlots to McGugin Field to the Nashville Sounds, he has left an indelible mark on the great game of baseball."

***

Bowie Kuhn, former commissioner of major league baseball: "One of the charms of baseball is the number of wonderful characters the game has produced. This is actually truer in the bushes than in the big-league version, though the latter are more publicized. Larry Schmittou is a genuine character. I don't know that he ever traded a ball player for a turkey, but I'll wager he thought about it. He did put AAA and AA clubs in the same park in the same season, and that alone gets him a Masters Degree in prestidigitation. He's a baseball traditionalist, chivalrous in the old Southern way, humorous, and smart enough to be rich—not that he's going to buy out any major Rockefellers, but he might pick off a grandnephew or two."

***

Jerry Cathey, Sounds assistant concession manager: "I first met Larry Schmittou in college in 1960 and have worked for him 17 years in various roles. He is a genuine and caring individual. He doesn't know the words We can't do that. And he expects his employees to have the same philosophy."

***

Fred Fisher, Thornton and Harwell Agency: "Larry Schmittou is a man who lives dreams many others only think about. It has been my opportunity to play sandlot baseball for him, to be recruited to Vanderbilt by him, and to play on an SEC baseball team for him. I have also worked on a business level with him. He has done more for Nashville than most give him credit for, and I still believe he will bring major baseball here one day."

***

Branch C. Rickey, president, American Association: "Since his entry into minor-league baseball, Larry Schmittou has continually been an influential and guiding force. He has impacted the way clubs across the country have promoted their teams and advanced the cause of minor-league baseball. He doesn't just promote baseball, he lives it."

***

Ted Giannoulas, the Famous San Diego Chicken: "Sir Larry is a principle figure in the renaissance of minor-league baseball in America. His vision of the game as both a developmental station of future baseball talent and a family entertainment are the hallmarks of his success. Larry was pro Nashville before it was cool to be pro Nashville."

***

Doris Taylor, Sounds secretary and game-day ticket seller: "I first met Larry Schmittou in 1978 and since then I have been impressed for these reasons: He is a workaholic but understanding when others cannot totally commit to his schedule; he is loyal and once you have earned his respect, you have a friend forever; he has principles and sticks to them; he is a true Southern gentleman; he is devoted to his family. I admire him for what he has accomplished, and I treasure our friendship."

***

Rick Renick, current Sounds manager: "Larry Schmittou is one of the finest men I have ever been associated with. He is supportive and he knows the game. Baseball is better because of Larry Schmittou."

***

Hoyt Wilhelm, New York Yankees farm-system pitching coach and Baseball Hall of Fame member: "Larry is a very knowledgeable baseball man, and in all my years in the game some of my most enjoyable ones were with the Sounds."

***

Jerry Riensdorf, owner of the Chicago White Sox and Chicago Bulls: "Larry Schmittou is a real hands-on minor-league owner. Running a minor-league team is a difficult task because your margins are so thin, but he has been very successful, due in large part to his creativity and hustle."

***

Mike Moore, president, National Association of Professional Baseball Leagues: "As the 1970's got underway, many 'experts' were reading minor-league baseball its last rites. Larry Schmittou was one of the men who arrived on the scene to breathe new life into the game. He has been a true leader and innovator."

***

Mike Mondelli, general sessions judge: "I have been acquainted with Larry Schmittou since the mid-1960's when I played for some of his teams. The Larry I knew back then has changed little from the Larry I know now; he is still a hard-driving, fierce competitor."

***

Don Mincher, former major-leaguer and GM of the Huntsville Stars: "Larry Schmittou proudly says his only hobby is his work in baseball, and he loves the game as much as anybody I know."

***

Jay Miller, former director of services for the Texas Rangers and current general manager of the New Orleans Baseball Club: "Larry Schmittou is everything good about baseball."

***

Bill Trickett, owner, Trickett Oldsmobile, and organizer of the 100 Club, of which Larry Schmittou and Johnny Cash are lifetime members: "I have wonderful memories of Larry Schmittou which go back to the days when he led the Vanderbilt baseball team to great heights. I will always be grateful for his friendship."

***

Joe (Black Cat) Reilly, legendary bat boy for over 50 years: "Larry is a nice person who will talk to anyone. If it wasn't for him, we wouldn't have baseball in Nashville."

***

John R. Reynolds, attorney, Nashville Sounds: "When I first met Larry in 1977, I knew his reputation as a football recruiter and baseball coach, but I knew nothing of his business acumen. I followed his advice to me: 'You take care of the legal work, and I'll take care of the business.' It has proven successful beyond imagination."

***

Gene Menees, former player for Vanderbilt and the Sounds and now an executive with the TSSAA: "Coach Schmittou is a man I greatly admire for what he has done for baseball, in Nashville, and for me personally."

***

Skeeter Barnes, ex-Sounds star, major-league player, and now coaching in Detroit Tigers farm system: "Larry and I have a mutual respect for each other because we have a common bond in our love for baseball."

***

Dave Kalich, executive director, American Baseball College Association: "Larry has been an outstanding leader, both at the college and professional level, in marketing and promoting baseball. Baseball as a whole is better today because of Larry's leadership."

***

Nathan Harlan, Sounds part-time employee: "I have been working for Mr. Schmittou for eight summers. He provided me a chance to continue my education by awarding me a scholarship. I owe him a great deal."

***

Richard Sterban, singer with the Oak Ridge Boys and early Sounds investor: "People have asked me what made me want to own a part of a minor-league baseball team. I have always told them it was not so much the team as it was the opportunity to work with Larry Schmittou. I had watched Larry coach at Vanderbilt and win SEC championships, and I knew he shared my love of baseball and knew the game. As a child I loved baseball, and Larry has allowed me to be a part of something I could only dream about—being an owner of a professional team."

***

Jerry Reed, entertainer and original Sounds investor: "Larry Schmittou is Nashville baseball. He brought baseball to Nashville, and thanks to him we can all enjoy the game today. I hope he realizes his dream of major-league baseball in the future. Of course, even then his life won't be complete until he can beat me in gin rummy—and that ain't gonna happen!"

***

Marge Schott, owner, Cincinnati Reds: "I've been in the world of the 'grand ole men of baseball' for 10 years. One person I think is a real businessman for baseball is Larry Schmittou, even though he is in the minor-league end of it. We had our AAA team in Nashville, but I didn't meet Larry for years. Then he showed up one day with his best asset, his wife, Shirley, and we immediately became friends. I knew he had to be a super guy to have such a great better half."

***

Pete Rose, baseball's all-time hit leader and former Cincinnati Reds manager: "Larry Schmittou has been great for baseball in Nashville, and his value will be even more in the major leagues someday."

***

Reese Smith III, one of the Sounds early investors: "Larry is the hardest-working partner with whom I've ever been associated. His main focus is family and baseball, baseball, baseball. He had no other real outside interests. He does not belong to a country club, does not play golf, hunt, or fish. All these things would be a distraction to Larry from attaining his goals. He can be hard-headed to a fault, but if he weren't so hard-headed, we would not have professional baseball in Nashville."

***

Bob Jamison, former Sounds announcer and California Angels announcer, whose young son tragically died one season: "When I think of Larry Schmittou, I think of my son, David. You find out who your friends are when you need help the most. During David's short life, there were many difficult and complicated times, and my wife, Susan, and I found that we were blessed with more friends than we knew we had. Larry was one of those who really came through for us. There were many games when I was physically at the game but my mind and heart were elsewhere, and I know that my broadcasts suffered as a result. It would have been justifiable for Larry to have made a change in announcers, but he didn't. He sympathized and stuck with me. There were times when schedules had to be altered and costly arrangements made, and these were never a problem, thanks to Larry Schmittou. He will always be a friend to me and my family."

***

Jim Turner, former major-league star, pitching coach for the New York Yankees, and Sounds fan: "Larry has a good personality. He made a smooth transition from amateur to professional baseball. He's a good baseball operator and has done a good job attracting fans. He is well respected in all of baseball."

***

Lorianne Crook, former Soundette and current TV personality: "My most vivid memory of Larry Schmittou is actually one that is embarrassing to me, but it shows how Larry has always been totally involved in his baseball park from the bottom up. I was a Soundette, one of a dozen girls who welcomed baseball fans into Greer Stadium, sold programs, took Cokes to the umpire, and so forth. Most of the time I was 15 to 20 minutes late getting to the ball park. So much was always going on in the stadium I didn't think anyone would notice. One day I was really late to a double-header. As I waltzed in behind the stands, Larry himself approached me and said, "You really need to be here on time if you want to do your job right." Then he walked on by. Needless to say, I was never late to another game, and I was very impressed that Larry was concerned about every single employee doing their absolute best to make the Nashville Sounds' games a great experience for fans."

***

Steve Carroll, former Sounds announcer, now in the National Hockey League: "The eight years I worked for Larry Schmittou I look at as a very pleasurable time. I have respect for him as to how he runs the team and his love and knowledge of the game of baseball. The thing I wanted to do was get better, and I think the job working with Nashville and Huntsvllle and working with a man that I could respect gave me the opportunity to be where I am today."

***

Brenard Wilson, former Vanderbilt and NFL star: "As one reflects back upon life, you realize that the Lord allows special people to come into your life. Coach Schmittou has been and is one of those special people in my life. From my teenage years at Vanderbilt to my adulthood, Coach Schmittou has had an impact upon the successes that I have enjoyed. I respect and admire him for what he has done and continues to do for people."

ABOUT THE AUTHOR

Larry Woody is a native of Crossville, Tennessee, who joined The Nashville *Tennessean* sports staff while attending Belmont College in 1967. Following a tour of duty in Vietnam where he won two citations for valor with the 199th Light Infantry Brigade, Woody returned to the *Tennessean,* where over the years he has covered auto racing, the NFL, and Southeastern Conference football and basketball.

A three-time *Tennessean* Sportswriter of the Year, Woody's stories have won several national awards, including one for his account of the tragic death of race-car driver Davey Allison. Woody contributes articles to numerous magazines and is the author of *A Dixie Farewell: The Life and Death of Chucky Mullins* and *Pure Sterling: The Sterling Marlin Story.* Woody resides in Nashville with his wife, Mary Frances, and their children, Susan, Hugh, and Brian.